STORYWORLDS Writing

Teaching Guide

STAGES 4–6

DEE REID AND DIANA BENTLEY

Heinemann

Authors
Dee Reid
Diana Bentley
Scottish correlation by Eleanor McMillan

Heinemann
Halley Court, Jordan Hill, Oxford OX2 8EJ
a division of Reed Educational and Professional Publishing Ltd
www.heinemann.co.uk
Heinemann is a registered trademark of Reed Educational and Professional Publishing Ltd

© Reed Educational and Professional Publishing Ltd, 2002

Storyworlds Writing Teaching Guide Stages 4–6
The material in this publication is copyright. The Photocopy Masters may be photocopied for one-time use as instructional material in a classroom, but they may not be copied in unlimited quantities, kept on behalf of others, passed on or sold to third parties, or stored for future use in a retrieval system. If you wish to use this material in any other way than that specified you must apply in writing to the Publisher.

0 435 15273 4

06 05 04 03 02
10 9 8 7 6 5 4 3 2 1

Acknowledgements
The Publisher would like to thank the following for permission to use copyright material in Storyworlds Writing.

Unit 1 Geraldine Kaye, author of the 'Red Ted' stories; Unit 2 Susan Akass, author of the 'Pirate Pete' stories; Unit 3 Nicola Moon, author of the 'Max' stories; Unit 4 Wes Magee, author of the 'Nesta and Ned' stories; Unit 5 James Riordan, for *The Wolf and the Kids*; Unit 10 Margaret Nash, for *The Gingerbread Man*.

Every effort has been made to obtain permission for copyright material. The Publisher would be grateful for any discrepancies to be notified.

Illustrated by Nicki Wise
Designed by bigtop, Bicester, UK
Printed in the UK by Ashford Colour Press

Contents

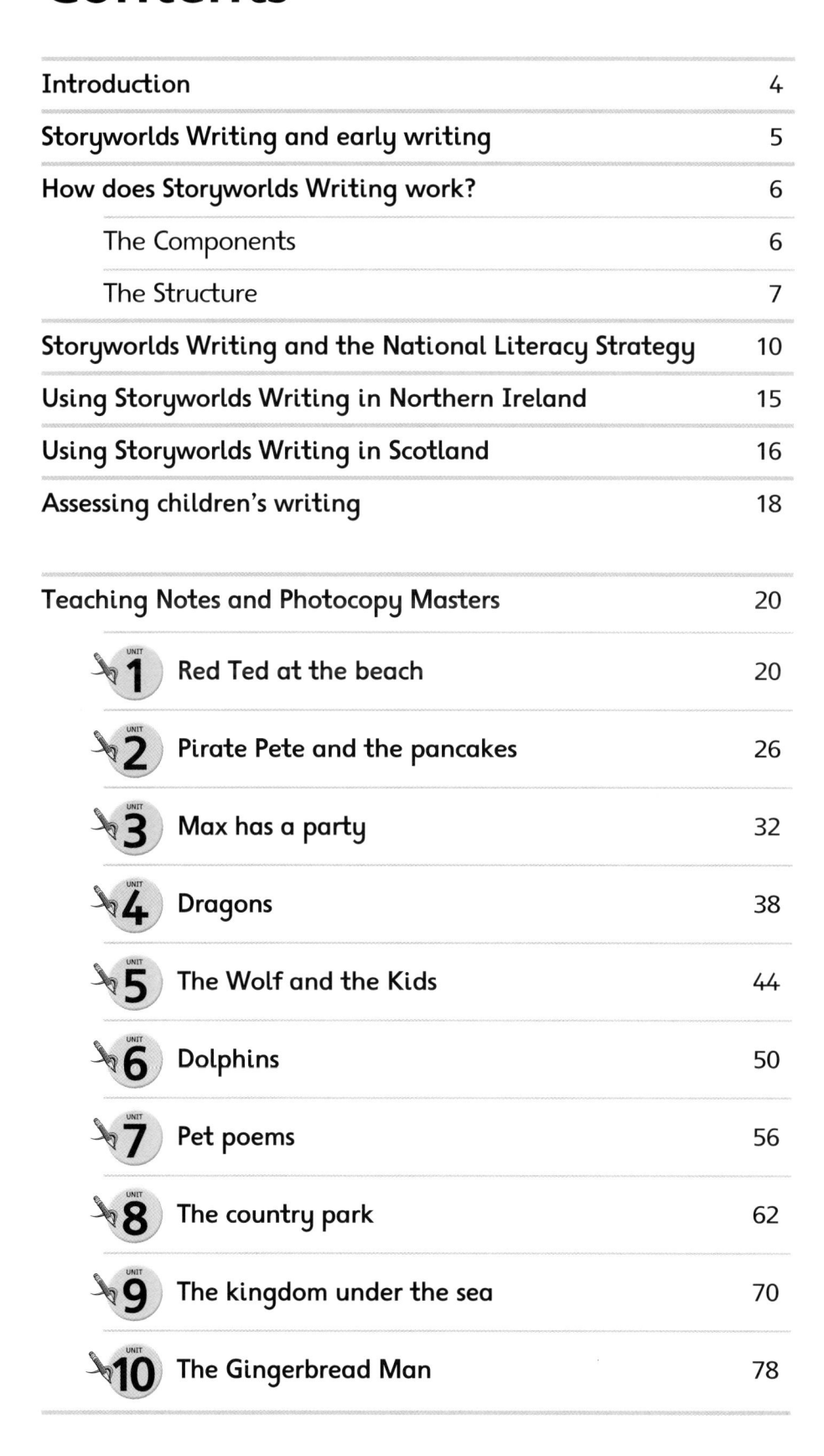

Introduction	4
Storyworlds Writing and early writing	5
How does Storyworlds Writing work?	6
The Components	6
The Structure	7
Storyworlds Writing and the National Literacy Strategy	10
Using Storyworlds Writing in Northern Ireland	15
Using Storyworlds Writing in Scotland	16
Assessing children's writing	18
Teaching Notes and Photocopy Masters	20
UNIT 1 Red Ted at the beach	20
UNIT 2 Pirate Pete and the pancakes	26
UNIT 3 Max has a party	32
UNIT 4 Dragons	38
UNIT 5 The Wolf and the Kids	44
UNIT 6 Dolphins	50
UNIT 7 Pet poems	56
UNIT 8 The country park	62
UNIT 9 The kingdom under the sea	70
UNIT 10 The Gingerbread Man	78

Introduction

Welcome to Storyworlds Writing

Storyworlds Writing is an exciting new writing programme especially designed to help you develop children's early writing skills from Foundation to Year 2. It provides a series of Big Book anthologies to encourage children to think actively about and enjoy writing, through model texts, stimulus illustrations and writing frames. A comprehensive Teaching Guide accompanies each Big Book and provides both lesson plans and photocopy masters.

If you use Storyworlds as your main reading resource, Storyworlds Writing will fit perfectly alongside it. We have selected some of the most popular characters and created scenarios that provide plenty of opportunities to develop children's writing. However, you do not need to have all the original Storyworlds books to use Storyworlds Writing effectively.

If you use resources other than Storyworlds for teaching reading, then Storyworlds Writing offers a complete, concise package for teaching writing. Storyworlds Writing can be used as a stand-alone resource, as all the stimulus material you need is in the Big Books, and the Teaching Guides offer comprehensive notes.

sample spread from Big Book Stages 4–6

Storyworlds Writing and early writing

It is important that any approach to writing encourages children in Key Stage 1 to explore and enjoy both the creative and physical process of writing. Storyworlds Writing does this by offering attractive and purposeful stimulus material that covers a range of contexts.

The importance of shared writing
Shared writing provides you with the opportunity to demonstrate the way that writers work. You can share with the children all the decisions that writers make and help them to shape everyday spoken language into appropriate language for writing. In shared writing you can work at a level beyond children's independent writing to develop and refine their ideas, and because they are not preoccupied with the transcriptional aspects of writing they can concentrate upon composition.

Developing Early Writing
Storyworlds Writing embraces the philosophy of the *Developing Early Writing* guidelines and enables the recommended approach to scaffolding writing to be followed.

Planning writing • whole class

Talk for writing
Each unit starts with a discussion to clarify the content and purpose of the writing and to 'tune children in' to the writing task. This phase of telling and re-telling enables teachers to share the overall structure of the writing task and to begin to shape it into 'writerly' language.

Making a plan
At this stage the teacher shares with the class an outline of the writing task they will be exploring. The intended text is recorded in note, picture or diagrammatic form. Teachers will refer to this plan when undertaking the writing tasks in subsequent sessions.

Shared writing • whole class / paired work

Shared writing consists of three clear stages:

Teacher demonstration
At this stage the teacher works from the 'talk for writing' to show how a text is written.

Teacher scribing
At this point in the session the teacher writes for the children while they compose and contribute all or some of the text.

Supported composition
At this stage the children have been adequately prepared for the writing task and are able to undertake aspects of the task individually or in pairs.

Independent but supported composition • independent / group work

For this, the children practise writing skills taught in the previous stages. They may add to, extend or complete work started in the shared task.

How does Storyworlds Writing work?

The Components

Year Group	Storyworlds Writing Stages		
Foundation/ Primary 1	Stages 1–3		
Year 1/ Primary 2	Stages 4–6		
Year 2/ Primary 3	Stages 7–9, & Bridges		

Storyworlds Writing Big Book Stages 4–6

The Big Book for Year 1/Primary 2 covers Storyworlds Writing Stages 4 to 6, and provides the stimulus for the shared writing activities. It covers the main fiction and poetry genres and non-fiction text types outlined in the National Literacy Strategy's *Framework for teaching*. The acetate sheets included with the Big Book enable you to demonstrate the writing process to the whole class.

Some pages are illustrations to spark children's imaginations. Some are illustrated stories to provide a model for children's writing. Others are 'writing pages' which provide a frame for story planning or for a non-fiction text type. There is a 'Writing review' page at the end of the Big Book, which you can use with children to discuss what they have learned and which units they have most enjoyed.

Storyworlds Writing Teaching Guide Stages 4–6

The Teaching Guide provides lesson plans and photocopy masters to support each unit. The lesson plans outline the relevant writing targets for the tasks and list the NLS writing objectives. They also provide all the details to run the units, including scripts for some of the 'teacher demonstration' activities.

Each unit has two photocopy masters to support children's writing. These are referenced in the group work section of some sessions and enable children to undertake writing tasks after these have been supported in shared work.

The Structure

The units
For Year 1/Primary 2 classes, there are ten units, which are linked to clusters of books from Storyworlds stages 4–6. These introduce fiction and non-fiction writing. In most of the fiction units, a key character from Storyworlds, such as the 'Gingerbread Man', is the focal point of a story writing activity. In the non-fiction units, the links to original Storyworlds may be based on a theme or topic, or simply provide the context for non-fiction writing. For example, there is a unit on writing simple instructions based on the 'Pirate Pete' character. The units cover the key Target Statements for Writing for Year 1.

How long should a unit last?
Each unit represents four literacy hours and may be completed in the course of a week. You may decide to spread the unit over two weeks allowing extra time for more groups of children to engage in the proposed group activities with adult support. Or, you may choose to run one or two of the sessions together to form an extended writing session, outside the literacy hour.

The sessions
Each unit is divided into four sessions. These sessions provide a sequence of activities which support the writing process through 'talk for writing', 'making a plan' into shared writing either by teacher demonstration or teacher scribing. All these build up to provide essential support for young writers, and by the end of each session, children should be participating in writing either in supported composition or independent work.

Each session starts with approximately 15 minutes of whole class shared work, using the Big Book.

The shared work is followed by a suggestion for group work. Sometimes this is independent work for children to undertake based on the teaching in the shared section of the session. Other times the group will need to work with an adult who can lead a discussion or role-play. As a general rule, photocopy masters provide the basis for group work for two out of the four sessions in any one unit.

Finally the session is concluded with a Rounding up time (10 minutes). In this time the teacher is able to revisit the key objectives of the session and the children have the opportunity to share work in progress.

Word level work
Each unit in Storyworlds Writing provides teacher support for 45 minutes of four literacy hours. Although many sessions have suggestions for 'applied' word level work in phonics and spelling, it is assumed that 15 minutes of 'pure' word level work (following the Progression in Phonics activities) will run alongside Storyworlds Writing.

A unit in detail

Introduction
an overview of the theme of the unit explaining its genre

Talk for writing
most units start with this important preparation for writing

TARGET
based on NLS writing targets

PUPIL TARGET
child-friendly language to focus learning

NLS OBJECTIVES
each unit addresses a number of objectives for the relevant year. These are predominantly text level objectives but, where appropriate, sentence and word level objectives are linked

SCOTTISH 5–14 GUIDELINES

OUTCOME
specific expectation that writing has a purpose and a goal

UNIT 3

Max has a party
List and invitation

Introduction
In this unit, children discuss the planning for a party and write an invitation.

Linked text: 'Max and the cat' (Big Book).

TARGET
- assemble ideas as a basis for writing

PUPIL TARGET
- I can write an invitation

OUTCOME
- a party invitation
- a 'Things to do' list

NLS OBJECTIVES

Y1 T1 T15	to make simple lists for planning
Y1 T1 S9	to use a capital letter for the personal pronoun 'I'
Y1 T1 W3	to practise and secure the ability to hear initial and final phonemes in CVC words
Y1 T1 W11	to spell common irregular words from Appendix List 1

SCOTTISH 5–14 GUIDELINES
- Functional writing
- Personal writing
- Spelling
- Handwriting and presentation

32

Session 1

You will need
- Big Book pages 10–11
- Flip chart and marker pen
- Acetate sheet

the animals have brought presents to the party

Talk for writing
- Show the children the Big Book pages 10–11. Explain that it is Max the mouse's birthday and he has invited all his friends to come to his party.
- Talk about the parties that the children have been to. Discuss what kind of special party food they have at parties.

Shared writing
Teacher demonstration
- Point to the different foods that are on the table in the picture and ask the children which friend they think will eat each food.
- Write their answers on the flip chart, talking through the writing process.

> Yes, the rabbit would like the grass. So I will write, 'The rabbit wants to eat the grass.'

- Continue asking for suggestions for Pecky (worms), Max (cheese) and write the sentences following the pattern above.
- Point to the presents that the friends have brought to the party.

> What should Max say to his friends when they give him their present? That's right, "Thank you very much." I will write that in the speech bubble.

Group work
- Ask the children to work with a partner and to decide what food the frog would like (flies) and what food the squirrel would like (nuts). Ask them to take it in turns to write a sentence for the frog and the squirrel.

Rounding up
- Tell the children that you are going to say a letter sound. Ask them to see if they can find something that starts or ends with that letter sound in the picture, e.g. m (mouse), d (duck), ch (cheese), b (ball), etc.

Session
each session has a shared component, a group/independent element and time for rounding up

You will need
a quick glance will indicate what resources are needed for each session

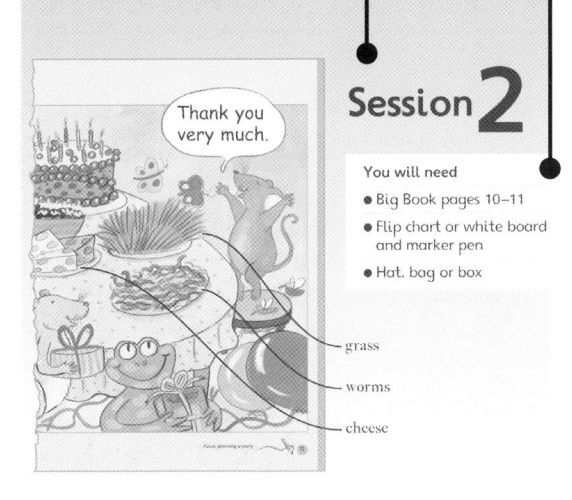

Session 2

UNIT 3 Max has a party

You will need
- Big Book pages 10–11
- Flip chart or white board and marker pen
- Hat, bag or box

Making a plan
Teacher scribing
- Ask the children if any of them is going to have a birthday soon. Will they have a party? Ask the class to help to plan a pretend party.
- Look at the picture on Big Book pages 10–11 and ask the children to think about what Max had to do before his party. Scribe their suggestions under a 'Things to do' list on the flip chart.

> Max has invited all his friends. We'll need to do that too, so I'll write, 'Make a list of all my friends' on my 'Things to do' list. We'll need to let them know the day and the time, so I'd better write some invitations. What else has Max done that we'll need to do? Yes, he's made lots of food and organised games to play, so we'll add those to the list.

Group work
- Ask the children to make a list of forfeits as party games, e.g. count from number ten backwards, clap your hands behind your back, hop round a table. (Adult help required.)

Rounding up
- Play 'forfeits' using the suggestions from the group work. Place the forfeits in a hat, bag or box and invite individual children to come out, take a forfeit and perform the instruction.

33

Making a plan
the teacher shares with the class an outline of the writing task

Group work
is based on the focus of the shared work. It can be tackled independently or by a group of children with or without adult support. Every unit has two photocopy masters to support children's independent writing

Rounding up
a plenary drawing together the teaching focus of the session and allowing time for reflection and evaluation

Differentiation
Differentiation in Storyworlds Writing is achieved primarily by outcome. All children at their individual levels of ability can tackle the activities suggested in the whole class activities. Differentiation by task is evident in the group work tasks, many of which have optional activities to challenge more able pupils.

Storyworlds Writing and the National Literacy Strategy

Matching the range

This table shows which genres and text types are covered by Storyworlds Writing Stages 4–6.

Unit		Range
1	Red Ted at the beach	Story with familiar setting
2	Pirate Pete and the pancakes	Instructions
3	Max has a party	List and invitation
4	Dragons	Poem with patterned language
5	The Wolf and the Kids	Traditional story
6	Dolphins	Non-chronological report
7	Pet poems	Poems on similar themes
8	The country park	Recount and information text
9	The kingdom under the sea	Story about a fantasy world
10	The Gingerbread Man	Traditional story

Medium-term planning for Year 1

Matching the target statements for writing

NLS Target statements for writing	Unit 1 Red Ted at the beach	Unit 2 Pirate Pete and the pancakes	Unit 3 Max has a party	Unit 4 Dragons	Unit 5 The Wolf and the Kids	Unit 6 Dolphins	Unit 7 Pet poems	Unit 8 The country park	Unit 9 The kingdom under the sea	Unit 10 The Gingerbread Man
Phonics and spelling										
• spell words with adjacent consonants	✎									
• spell unfamiliar words using a phonemic strategy		✎	✎	✎			✎	✎		✎
• know main spelling choices for each vowel phoneme										
• spell 50 words from high-frequency word list										
Handwriting										
• form lower case letters correctly in a script that will be easy to join later										
Style: language effects										
• begin to use words appropriate to different text forms	✎	✎		✎	✎		✎			✎
Style: sentence construction										
• write simple sentences independently	✎	✎	✎	✎	✎	✎		✎	✎	✎
• write questions and statements appropriately		✎	✎	✎	✎	✎	✎	✎	✎	✎
Punctuation										
• use capital letters and full stops when punctuating a single simple sentence	✎	✎	✎	✎	✎	✎		✎	✎	✎
• begin to use question marks										
Purpose and organisation										
• write a recount or narrative	✎		✎	✎	✎	✎		✎	✎	✎
• write to communicate meaning										
• write simple instructions in correct order										
• label information appropriately										
Process										
• use language and structures from reading when writing	✎	✎	✎	✎		✎	✎	✎	✎	✎
• assemble information and ideas from own experience as a basis for writing										
• begin to rehearse sentences before writing										

Medium-term planning for Year 1

Matching the writing objectives

Year 1 Term 1 NLS Writing Objectives	Unit 1 Red Ted at the beach	Unit 2 Pirate Pete and the pancakes	Unit 3 Max has a party
Term 1 Fiction writing composition			
Y1 T1 T8 — to apply phonological, graphic knowledge and sight vocabulary to spell words	✎		
Y1 T1 T10 — to use rhymes and patterned stories as models for their own writing			
Y1 T1 T11 — to make simple picture storybooks	✎		
Term 1 Non-fiction writing composition			
Y1 T1 T14 — to write captions for their own work	✎		✎
Y1 T1 T15 — to make simple lists			✎
Y1 T1 T16 — to write and draw simple instructions		✎	
Cross references to other objectives	S6, S8, W4	S4, S9, W12	T1, S9, W3, W11

Key

✎ = specifically targeted

= covered in general teaching

Year 1 Term 2 NLS Writing Objectives		UNIT 4 Dragons	UNIT 5 The Wolf and the Kids	UNIT 6 Dolphins
Term 2 Fiction writing composition				
Y1 T2 T12	to apply phonological, graphic knowledge and sight vocabulary to spell words			
Y1 T2 T13	to substitute and extend patterns through language play	✎		
Y1 T2 T14	to represent outlines of story plots		✎	
Y1 T2 T15	to build simple character profiles	✎		
Y1 T2 T16	to use elements of stories in own writing		✎	
Term 2 Non-fiction writing composition				
Y1 T2 T22	to write labels for drawings and diagrams			✎
Y1 T2 T23	to produce extended captions		✎	
Y1 T2 T24	to write simple questions			✎
Y1 T2 T25	to assemble information; to use simple sentences; to write simple reports and lists			✎
Cross references to other objectives		T11	T10, S5, S6	S6, W7

Key

✎ = specifically targeted

= covered in general teaching

STORYWORLDS Writing

Year 1 Term 3 NLS Writing Objectives		UNIT 7 Pet poems	UNIT 8 The country park	UNIT 9 The kingdom under the sea	UNIT 10 The Gingerbread Man
Term 3 Fiction writing composition					
Y1 T3 T12	to apply phonological, graphic knowledge and sight vocabulary to spell words			✒	
Y1 T3 T13	to write about significant incidents from known stories			✒	✒
Y1 T3 T14	to write stories using simple settings			✒	✒
Y1 T3 T15	to use poems as models for own writing	✒			
Y1 T3 T16	to compose own poetic sentences	✒			
Term 3 Non-fiction writing composition					
Y1 T3 T20	to write simple recounts		✒		
Y1 T3 T21	to use the language and features of non-fiction texts		✒		
Y1 T3 T22	to write own questions prior to reading				
Cross references to other objectives			S5 W1		

Key

✒ = specifically targeted

☐ = covered in general teaching

Using Storyworlds Writing in Northern Ireland

The approach taken in Storyworlds fits in with many aspects of the Programme of Study for English for Key Stage 1. Storyworlds Writing Stages 4–6 aims to cover Level 1 and elements of Level 2.

Progression
There is an emphasis on scaffolding the writing process for children through the teacher demonstrating, scribing and supported composition during the shared writing session. This enables children to progress from expressing ideas for the teacher to write, towards writing with some independence.

Planning
In Storyworlds Writing, children are actively encouraged to talk about their writing both with the whole class and in group work. There are many structured opportunities for discussion, organising ideas and making plans before writing.

Purpose and Range
Storyworlds Writing provides the opportunities to write in the following forms.

Unit		Range	Purpose
1	Red Ted at the beach	story	express thoughts and imaginings
2	Pirate Pete and the pancakes	story, information material	inform and explain
3	Max has a party	story, information material	inform and explain
4	Dragons	poems	describe, express thoughts and imaginings
5	The Wolf and the Kids	story	narrate, express thoughts and imaginings
6	Dolphins	information material	report, record findings
7	Pet Poems	poems	describe, express thoughts and imaginings
8	The country park	information leaflet	describe, inform and explain
9	The kingdom under the sea	story	narrate, express thoughts and imaginings
10	The Gingerbread Man	story	narrate, express thoughts and imaginings

Using Storyworlds Writing in Scotland

The National Guidelines for English Language 5-14 recommend that children practise three types of writing: functional writing or writing for a simple practical purpose (such as instructions), personal writing or writing about a personal experience using words which express feelings, and imaginative writing such as a brief story.

Although the 5-14 strands in Storyworlds Writing are related to the writing mode of the language guidelines, there are opportunities to develop listening, talking and reading.

In the suggested class lessons, where the teacher is demonstrating the writing process, advantage should be taken to talk about texts and consider the writer's ideas and craft.

At every stage, the teacher is encouraging pupils to organise their thinking and ideas in order to plan, draft and re-draft what they want to write. This approach, therefore, provides incidental opportunities to investigate language and the use of language in more detail.

Storyworlds Writing will enrich and extend any reading programme and help teachers support pupils in making links between what they are reading and writing, which is an important feature identified in the HMI document Improving Writing 5-14.

Storyworlds Writing Stages 4-6 covers Level A of the 5-14 Scottish Guidelines.

Unit	Strand	Aspect
Unit 1 Red Ted at the beach	Personal writing	write briefly, expressing ideas
	Imaginative writing	compose simple sentence structures with the teacher acting as scribe: with teacher support, use a story plan to sequence the writing, discussing beginning, middle and end
	Punctuation and structure	use capital letters and full stops
	Spelling	use knowledge of phonological awareness
Unit 2 Pirate Pete and the pancakes	Imaginative writing	explore ideas through role-play
	Functional writing	with the teacher acting as scribe, select important features to order the writing; demonstrate and discuss the use of verbs at the beginning of each instruction
	Handwriting and presentation	discuss the layout of instructions and the use of numbering to show sequence
Unit 3 Max has a party	Functional writing	through modelling and careful questioning, the teacher will help pupils make a simple list; use a simple frame to write an invitation
	Personal writing	write briefly, expressing own ideas
	Spelling	use knowledge of phonological awareness and common words
	Handwriting and presentation	write legibly giving attention to correct letter formation
Unit 4 Dragons	Imaginative writing	consider character through drawings, develop use of adjectives when describing character; using a simple poem as a framework, the teacher will scribe pupils' suggestions, discussing how they can refine their ideas: consider rhyme and rhythm in poetry writing
	Spelling	use knowledge of phonological awareness
	Handwriting and presentation	write legibly giving attention to correct letter formation

Unit	Strand	Aspect
UNIT 5 The Wolf and the Kids	Imaginative writing	develop ideas through role-play; with teacher support, consider character and setting; with teacher acting as scribe, use a story plan to sequence the writing, discussing beginning, middle and end
	Punctuation and structure	use capital letters and full stops appropriately
UNIT 6 Dolphins	Functional writing	with teacher support, formulate questions; with the teacher modelling, look at labelling and discuss the importance of this strategy in functional writing; through modelling and careful questioning, help pupils make simple notes using headings and bullet points
	Handwriting and presentation	write legibly in an appropriate form
	Punctuation and structure	use capital letters, full stops and question marks
UNIT 7 Pet poems	Functional writing	with teacher support, write a list
	Personal writing	write briefly, expressing own ideas
	Imaginative writing	using a simple poem as a framework, the teacher will scribe pupils' suggestions, discussing how they can refine their ideas
	Spelling	use knowledge of rhyme and alliteration
	Handwriting and presentation	write legibly giving attention to correct letter formation
UNIT 8 The country park	Functional writing	simple labelling; with teacher support, use a diagram to sequence writing; through modelling and careful questioning, help pupils to make simple notes, using headings and bullet points; use notes to order writing
	Spelling	use knowledge of phonological awareness
	Handwriting and presentation	write legibly in an appropriate form
UNIT 9 The kingdom under the sea	Imaginative writing	with teacher support, consider character and setting; develop ideas through role-play; with teacher support, use pictures to sequence the story, discussing beginning, middle and end
	Punctuation and structure	use capital letters and full stops appropriately
	Spelling	use phonological awareness
UNIT 10 The Gingerbread Man	Imaginative writing	with teacher support, use pictures to sequence the story and consider character; through modelling, help pupils plan and write a simple story based on the framework of a traditional tale
	Punctuation and structure	use capital letters and full stops appropriately

Assessing children's writing

Effective assessment underpins focussed teaching. It enables the teacher to establish what a child can do and to identify future learning goals.

Each Storyworlds Writing unit builds towards an independent writing task that can be used for assessment purposes. The independent tasks are undertaken after teacher demonstration, teacher scribing and supported composition. The independent writing can be used to assess a child's growing competence in both composition (purpose and audience) and transcriptional (spelling and handwriting) skills.

Pupil Targets
Self-assessment forms an important part of the assessment procedure and even young writers can be encouraged to reflect upon achievements and challenges.

Each unit has a specific 'pupil target' to focus learning. It is suggested that this target should be discussed with the whole class and referred to during the course of the unit.

The Pupil Assessment Chart on page 19 enables teachers to record whole class achievement of the writing targets. It will also highlight areas where further teaching is necessary either for the class or groups of children.

Pupil Assessment Chart

Use this chart to record children's performance against the main writing target for each unit.

Names	UNIT 1 Red Ted at the beach write simple sentences independently	UNIT 2 Pirate Pete and the pancakes write simple instructions	UNIT 3 Max has a party assemble ideas as a basis for writing	UNIT 4 Dragons use language and structures from reading when writing	UNIT 5 The Wolf and the Kids write a story that can be re-read	UNIT 6 Dolphins use words appropriate to different text forms	UNIT 7 Pet poems write a poem	UNIT 8 The country park write a recount	UNIT 9 The kingdom under the sea write a story with basic beginning, middle and end	UNIT 10 The Gingerbread Man begin to rehearse sentences before writing

UNIT 1

Red Ted at the beach

Story with a familiar setting

Introduction

In this unit, children plot and sequence Red Ted's day at the beach and write a simple version of the story.

Linked text:
'Red Ted at the beach' (Big Book).

TARGET

- write simple sentences independently
- assemble ideas as a basis for writing
- write a narrative

PUPIL TARGET

- I can retell a story in sequential order and write captions

OUTCOME

- a story book

NLS OBJECTIVES

Y1 T1 T14	to write captions for their own work
Y1 T1 S6	to begin using the term *sentence* to identify sentences in text
Y1 T1 S8	to begin using full stops to demarcate sentences
Y1 T1 W4	to discriminate and segment all three phonemes in CVC words

SCOTTISH 5–14 GUIDELINES

- Personal writing
- Imaginative writing
- Punctuation and structure
- Spelling

Session 1

Red Ted at the beach

You will need

- Big Book pages 2–3
- Items from the seaside, e.g. postcards, sand
- Blu-Tack
- 2 sets of word cards for each group as follows: Lucy, Red Ted, ball, seagull, sea, sand
- Flip chart and marker pen

Talk for writing

- Talk about what you did in the holidays, and tell the children about a trip to the seaside. Show some of the things you have brought back, and ask the children to tell you what they look or feel like. Write their suggestions on the flip chart.

- Tell the children that they are going on an imaginary trip to the seaside. Tell them to walk through the crunchy sand (saying "crunch, crunch"); to walk along the edge of the water ("splash, splash"); to look into a pool and see a tiny crab (walk their hands sideways) and two small fish going in and out of the red and green seaweed (place palms together and move hands in a fish-like movement); to sit down and have a picnic (mime eating sandwiches); and to build a sandcastle (dig the sand and then pat it into shape).

- Show them the picture of the seaside in the Big Book and ask them to name all the things they can see. Draw attention to Red Ted on the rock and point out that he is Lucy's favourite teddy and that she has taken him with her to the seaside.

Group work

- Shuffle the word cards and spread them out face down on the table. Explain to the children that they should take it in turns to turn over two cards and try to collect matching pairs. If they find a matching pair they should keep them. The winner is the child with the most matching pairs.

- Ask the children to play a game of 'Memory' with the word cards.

Rounding up

- Using one set of the word cards, give out a card to pairs of children. Ask the children to label the stimulus picture in the Big Book.

Session 2

Red Ted at the beach

You will need
- Big Book pages 2–3
- Flip chart or white board and marker pen

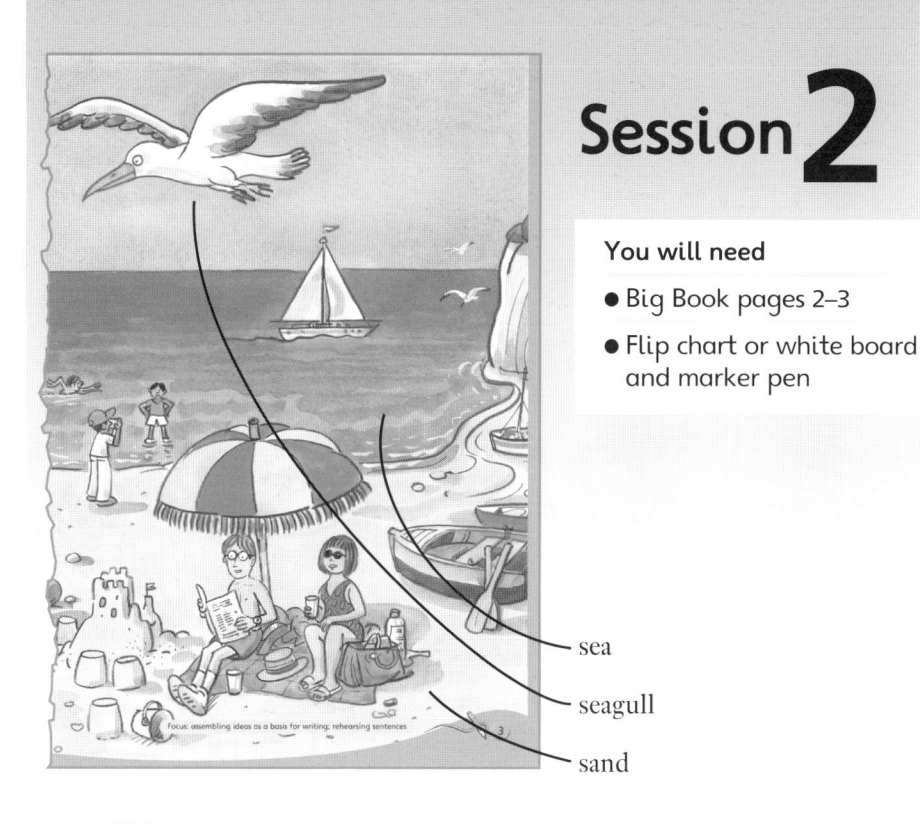

- sea
- seagull
- sand

Shared writing

Teacher scribing

- Show the class Big Book pages 2–3.

- Explain that they are going to help you to write some sentences. These sentences will help you to write a story about Red Ted and Lucy. Tell them to turn to their partner and to think of a sentence together to describe what's happening in the picture.

- Talk through the writing process as you scribe one of their sentences on the flip chart, e.g.

  > What must I remember to start my sentence with? That's right, it needs a capital letter. I am going to write, 'The seagull is flying in the sky.' How many words are there in my sentence? Let's count them together.

- Scribe some more of their sentences, helping them to revise their suggestions if they are not complete sentences. Remind them that all sentences need a full stop at the end.

Group work

- Ask the children to choose something they would like to do at the seaside. They should draw a picture and write a sentence under it, e.g. 'I like swimming in the sea.'

Rounding up

- Look together at some of the sentences the children have written. Draw attention to the capital letters and full stops.

UNIT 1
Red Ted at the beach

Session 3

You will need

- Big Book pages 4–5
- 2 pieces of card with 'yes' and 'no' on them for each child
- Copies of PCM 1
- Flip chart and marker pen

beginning

middle

1	Lucy put Red Ted on a rock.
2	The seagull swooped down and took Red Ted away.
3	The seagull dropped Red Ted into her nest.

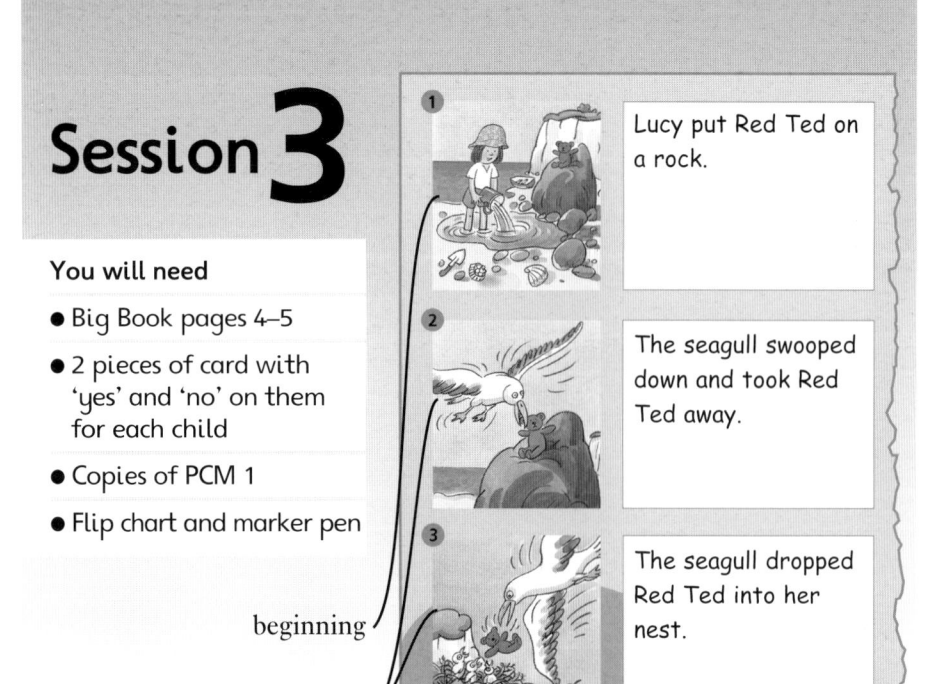

Shared writing/Making a plan

Teacher demonstration

- Show the class Big Book pages 4–5 and go through the story strip ensuring the children follow the pattern of events.
- Explain to the class that you are going to write a plan for the story of 'Red Ted at the beach'.
- Draw three sections onto the flip chart and label them – 'Beginning', 'Middle', 'End'. Discuss which pictures form the beginning, middle and end of the story.
- Ask the children what happened first (Red Ted was put on a rock). Write the sentence into the first section and talk about the features of the writing.

> How many words are there in our sentence? Now, I must start with a capital letter. What do I need at the end of a sentence?

- Ask them to help you to complete the story plan, suggesting sentences for the beginning, middle and end of the story. Talk through the writing process.

Group work

- PCM 1 Ask the children to write a sentence under each of the headings – 'Beginning', 'Middle', 'End'.

Rounding up

- Give each child two small pieces of card with the words 'yes' and 'no' written on them. Explain that you are going to ask some questions and they should work with a partner to decide if the answer is 'yes' or 'no'.

> Did Red Ted go to the seaside? Did he have a ride on a shark? Was he put into a seagull's nest? Did Sam rescue Red Ted?

- Ask the children to support their answers by referring to evidence in the Big Book.

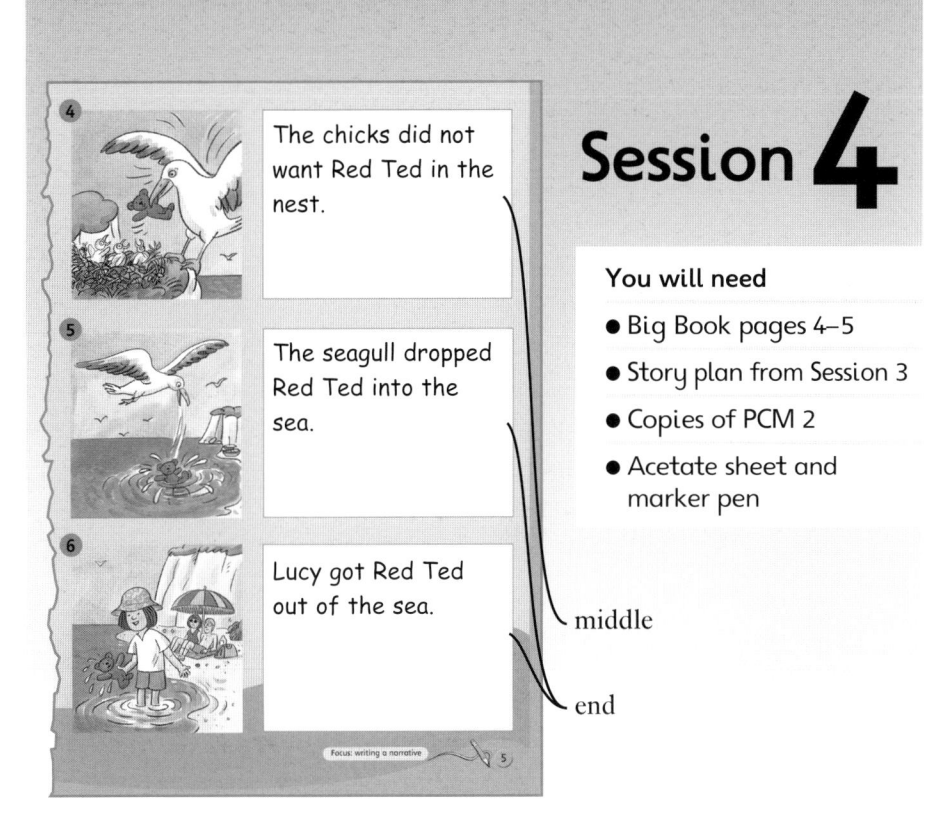

Session 4

Panel 4: The chicks did not want Red Ted in the nest.

Panel 5: The seagull dropped Red Ted into the sea. — middle

Panel 6: Lucy got Red Ted out of the sea. — end

You will need
- Big Book pages 4–5
- Story plan from Session 3
- Copies of PCM 2
- Acetate sheet and marker pen

Shared writing

Teacher demonstration

- Recap the story of 'Red Ted at the beach' and tell the children that you are going to use the story plan and the pictures to write the story in the Big Book.
- Point to the plan and read the first section. Write the story on the acetate sheet.

> I am going to start our story by writing, 'One day, Lucy took Red Ted to the beach. She put him on a rock while she played in a rock pool.' That's a good start, now what happened next? Let's see what our plan said. Oh dear, the seagull came and took Red Ted away. Now I'll write about that. This is the next section – the middle. 'A big seagull swooped down and picked up Red Ted in her beak. She flew back to her nest and dropped Red Ted into the nest, but the chicks did not want Red Ted.' Now we come to the end of the story. So what did the story plan say? That's right, the seagull drops Red Ted into the sea where Lucy finds him. So I will write, 'The seagull flew off again with Red Ted. She opened her beak and he fell down, down, down into the sea with a big splash. "What are you doing in the sea?" said Lucy and she put Red Ted back on the rock.'

Group work

- PCM 2 Enlarge the PCM to A3 size. It has six pictures on it with space underneath for the children to write captions. The PCM can then be folded to become a zig-zag book showing the story. If necessary, support their writing by using a highlighter pen for the child to write over.

Rounding up

- Ask the children to share the work on the zig-zag books from their group work. Talk about what you would need to put on the cover.

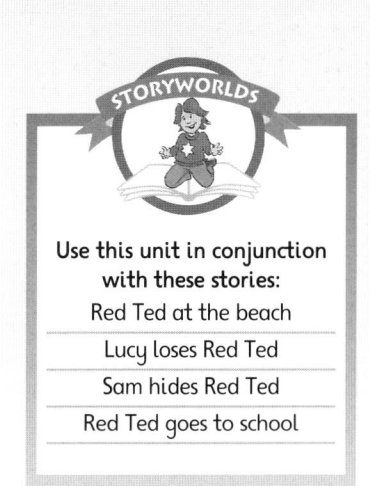

UNIT 1 — Red Ted at the beach

STORYWORLDS

Use this unit in conjunction with these stories:
- Red Ted at the beach
- Lucy loses Red Ted
- Sam hides Red Ted
- Red Ted goes to school

Name _____

Red Ted at the beach

Write a sentence for each heading.

Beginning

Lucy

Middle

Red Ted

End

rock

seagull   nest   sea

Name

What happened to Red Ted?

Write what happens in each picture.

Unit 1 Red Ted at the beach (Session 4) • **Skill:** writing a book
Enlarge the PCM to A3 size. Ask the children to write what happens in each picture.
Help the children to make a zig-zag book.

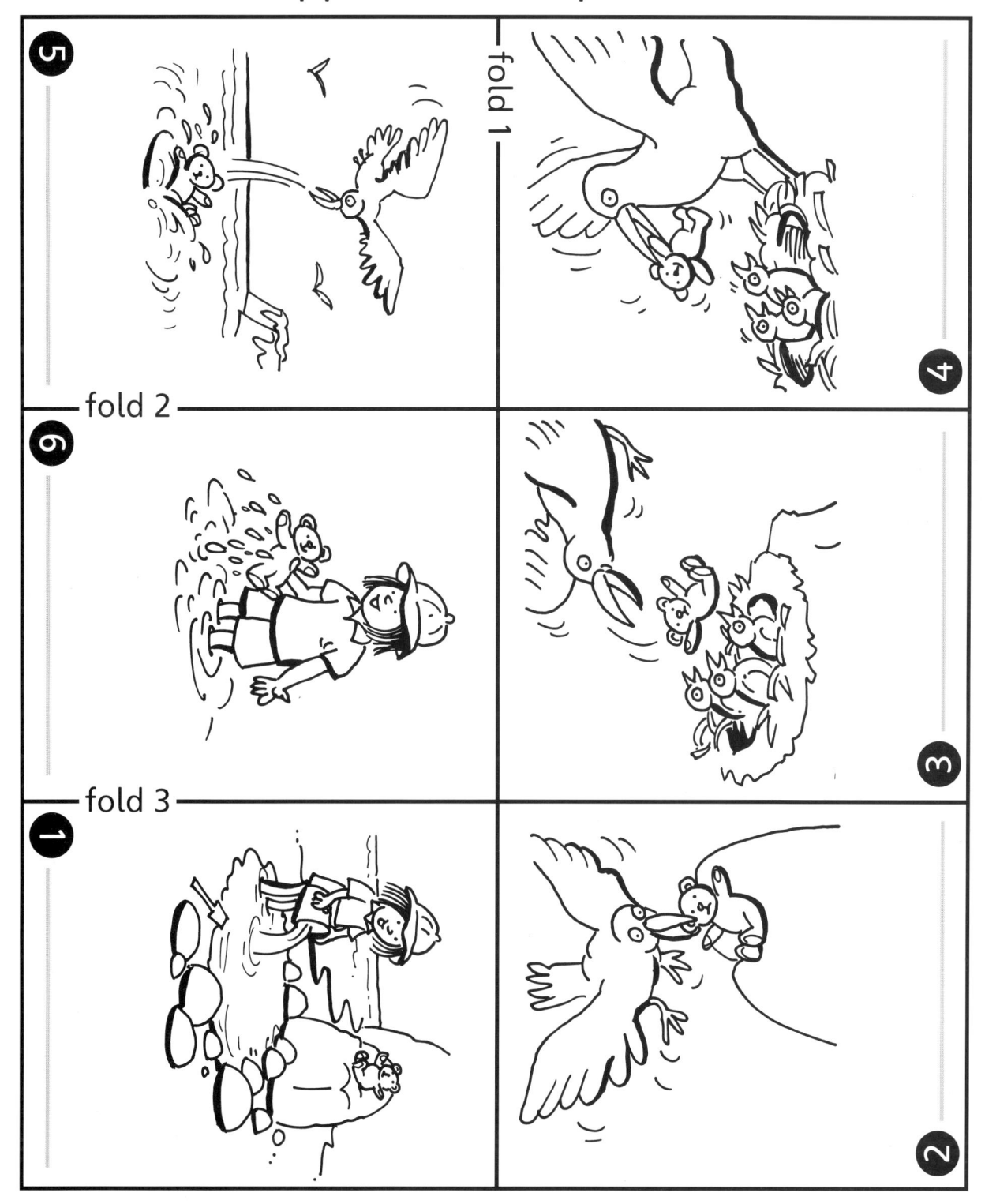

UNIT 2

Pirate Pete and the pancakes
Instructions

Introduction
In this unit, children write instructions for making pancakes.

Linked text:
'Pirate Pete and the monster' (Big Book).

TARGET
- write simple instructions
- use words appropriate to different text forms, e.g. story, instructions

PUPIL TARGET
- I can write instructions

OUTCOME
- instructions for making pancakes

NLS OBJECTIVES

Y1 T1 T16	to write and draw simple instructions
Y1 T1 S4	to write captions and simple sentences
Y1 T1 S9	to use a capital letter for the start of a sentence
Y1 T1 W12	new words from shared experiences, to make collections of words linked to particular topics

SCOTTISH 5–14 GUIDELINES
- Imaginative writing
- Functional writing
- Handwriting and presentation

Session 1

You will need
- Big Book pages 6–7
- 8 small pieces of card in the shape of speech bubbles
- Blu-Tack
- Marker pen

examples for speech bubbles:
Beaky: I will make some pancakes for our tea.
Pirate Pete: That's a good idea.

> **Pirate Pete and the pancakes**
>
> Beaky was making some pancakes. He put some flour, an egg and some milk into a bowl, and mixed them all together.
>
> He poured the mixture into a frying pan.

Talk for writing
- Show the class the Big Book pages 6–7.
- Read the story about Pirate Pete to the class, pointing at the words as you read.
- Ask the class if they have ever eaten a pancake. Did they like it? What did they put on the pancake? Have they ever seen anyone toss a pancake?

Teacher demonstration
- Explain to the class that you want to write the words that Pirate Pete and Beaky might be saying onto speech bubbles. Write the children's suggestions on the cards, talking through the writing process as you write.

> What does Beaky say first? Yes, that's a good suggestion. Beaky said, "I will make some pancakes for our tea." What should I start my sentence with? What must I put at the end of the sentence? What does Pirate Pete say? Yes, he said, "That's a good idea." What shall we write for the next picture? What do you think Beaky said next?

- End the story with Pirate Pete saying his catchphrase, "Thundering Cannonballs!"

Group work
- Ask the children to role-play the story with adult help, using the work from the shared session as prompts.

Rounding up
- Give out the speech bubbles to pairs of children. Ask them to try to read the speech bubble and to decide from where in the story it comes.
- Then ask the children to come out and ask one child to read the speech bubble and the other child to put it in the right place in the book.

UNIT 2

Pirate Pete and the pancakes

Session 2

When the pancake was nearly cooked, Beaky tossed it high into the air...

and the pancake landed right on Pirate Pete's head.

You will need

- Big Book pages 6–7
- Small frying pan (optional)
- 1 cardboard pancake for tossing in the pan (optional)
- Flip chart and marker pen

Making a plan

- Recap the story with the children, and ask them to help you to work out how to make pancakes.

  > What is Beaky using to make the pancakes? That's right, flour, an egg and milk. What does he put into the bowl first? That's right, the flour. What do you think he puts in next? Yes, he must break the egg and put it in. Then he puts in the milk. Then what does he do? Yes, he stirs the mixture. Then what does he do? What does he do at the end? That's right, he tosses the pancakes.

- On the flip chart, make simple notes to summarise the process as you go, e.g.
  1. Find ingredients.
  2. Mix them in a bowl.
  3. Pour into pan and cook it.
  4. Toss it.

Group work

- Ask the children to take it in turns to mime one of the actions for making a pancake. The rest of the group should identify the action.

Rounding up

- Tell the children they are to take it in turns to try tossing a cardboard pancake and catching it in the pan.
- Alternatively, ask the children if they can remind you what you need to make a pancake and what you should do to cook it.

UNIT 2
Pirate Pete and the pancakes

Session 3

You will need
- Big Book page 8
- Copies of PCM 3
- Acetate sheet and marker pen

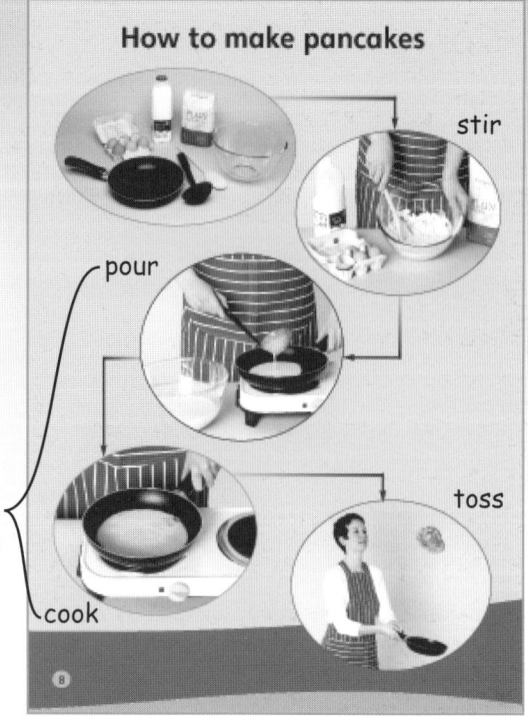

How to make pancakes

examples of verbs in instructions: stir, pour, toss, cook

Talk for writing

- Look at the photographs on page 8 of the Big Book with the children. Ask them what the photographs tell you. Is it easier to understand how to make a pancake from this page, rather than by reading the story about Pirate Pete and Beaky?

Making a plan

- Tell the children that you are going to write some notes about how to make pancakes. Ask the children to look at the pictures and to make suggestions for words to use. Scribe these on the acetate.
- Talk about verbs in instructions and ask the children to suggest a verb for each picture.

Group work

- PCM 3 Ask the children to put in the correct instruction words.

Rounding up

- Teach the children the following rhyme, and ask them to do the actions.

> 'Mix the pancake,
> Stir the pancake,
> Pop it in the pan.
> Fry the pancake,
> Toss the pancake,
> Catch it if you can.'

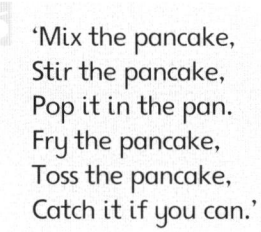

(*by* Christina Rossetti)

Session 4

UNIT 2
Pirate Pete and the pancakes

> **How to make pancakes**
> You will need:
> flour, milk, an egg, a bowl,
> a spoon, a ladle, a frying pan.
> What to do:
> 1. Put the flour into the bowl.
> 2. Add the egg and the milk.
> 3. Stir the ingredients together.
> 4. Pour some mixture into the pan.
> 5. Cook the pancake.
> 6. Toss the pancake.
> Enjoy your pancake!

— Simple instructions

You will need
- Big Book pages 8–9
- Copies of PCM 4
- Acetate sheet and marker pen

Shared writing

Teacher demonstration

- Explain that now you want to write some more detailed instructions for making pancakes and ask the children to remind you of the first thing to do. Use page 8 in the Big Book to prompt the children.

- Write the instructions on the frame on page 9 of the Big Book, e.g.

   > So if I want other people to make pancakes I must tell them what to do. So I will write the first instruction, 'Put the flour into the bowl.' Then what should they do? That's right, they should add the egg and the milk. So I will write, 'Add the egg and the milk.'

- Continue to write the instructions on the frame, e.g. 'Stir the ingredients together. Pour a little of the mixture into the pan. Cook the pancake. Toss the pancake.'

- Ask the children to read through the instructions and point out to them how you have started each sentence with a verb that tells you what to do.

Group work

- PCM 4 Ask the children to write the instructions for making a pancake. If necessary, support the children by writing in highlighter pen for them to write over.

Rounding up

- Using the instructions you have completed on page 9 of the Big Book, ask the children to point out the features of good instructions (numbered steps, starting with verbs, list of what you need, etc.).

STORYWORLDS

Use this unit in conjunction with these stories:
Pirate Pete and the monster
Pirate Pete loses his hat
Pirate Pete and the treasure island
Pirate Pete keeps fit

DISCOVERY WORLD

Fun Things to Make and Do (instructions)
Breakfast (explanation)

Name _____

A pancake recipe

Fill in the gaps using the words in the box.

> Stir   Put   Eat   Cook   Toss   Pour

How to make a pancake

You will need:

80g flour	bowl
1 egg	spoon
150ml milk	ladle
	frying pan

What to do

_____ the ingredients into the bowl.

_____ the mixture until it is smooth.

_____ the mixture into the frying pan.

_____ the pancake.

_____ the pancake and catch it in the pan.

_____ the pancake with jam and sugar.

Name _____

How to make a pancake

Write the instructions for making a pancake.

You will need:

_____   _____

_____   _____

_____

_____

What to do:

1 _____

2 _____

3 _____

4 _____

5 _____

6 _____

Enjoy your pancake!

- flour
- egg
- milk
- bowl
- spoon
- ladle
- frying pan

Stir
Put
Cook
Pour
Toss
Add

Unit 2 Pirate Pete and the pancakes (Session 4) • **Skill:** writing a recipe
Ask the children to write the instructions for making a pancake. Support the children if necessary by writing in highlighter pen for them to write over.

UNIT 3

Max has a party
List and invitation

Introduction

In this unit, children discuss the planning for a party and write an invitation.

Linked text: 'Max and the cat' (Big Book).

TARGET
- assemble ideas as a basis for writing

PUPIL TARGET
- I can write an invitation

OUTCOME
- a party invitation
- a 'Things to do' list

NLS OBJECTIVES

Y1 T1 T15	to make simple lists for planning
Y1 T1 S9	to use a capital letter for the personal pronoun 'I'
Y1 T1 W3	to practise and secure the ability to hear initial and final phonemes in CVC words
Y1 T1 W11	to spell common irregular words from Appendix List 1

SCOTTISH 5–14 GUIDELINES
- Functional writing
- Personal writing
- Spelling
- Handwriting and presentation

Session 1

You will need
- Big Book pages 10–11
- Flip chart and marker pen
- Acetate sheet

the animals have brought presents to the party

Talk for writing

- Show the children the Big Book pages 10–11. Explain that it is Max the mouse's birthday and he has invited all his friends to come to his party.
- Talk about the parties that the children have been to. Discuss what kind of special party food they have at parties.

Shared writing

Teacher demonstration

- Point to the different foods that are on the table in the picture and ask the children which friend they think will eat each food.
- Write their answers on the flip chart, talking through the writing process.

> Yes, the rabbit would like the grass. So I will write, 'The rabbit wants to eat the grass.'

- Continue asking for suggestions for Pecky (worms), Max (cheese) and write the sentences following the pattern above.
- Point to the presents that the friends have brought to the party.

> What should Max say to his friends when they give him their present? That's right, "Thank you very much." I will write that in the speech bubble.

Group work

- Ask the children to work with a partner and to decide what food the frog would like (flies) and what food the squirrel would like (nuts). Ask them to take it in turns to write a sentence for the frog and the squirrel.

Rounding up

- Tell the children that you are going to say a letter sound. Ask them to see if they can find something that starts or ends with that letter sound in the picture, e.g. m (mouse), d (duck), ch (cheese), b (ball), etc.

Session 2

You will need
- Big Book pages 10–11
- Flip chart or white board and marker pen
- Hat, bag or box

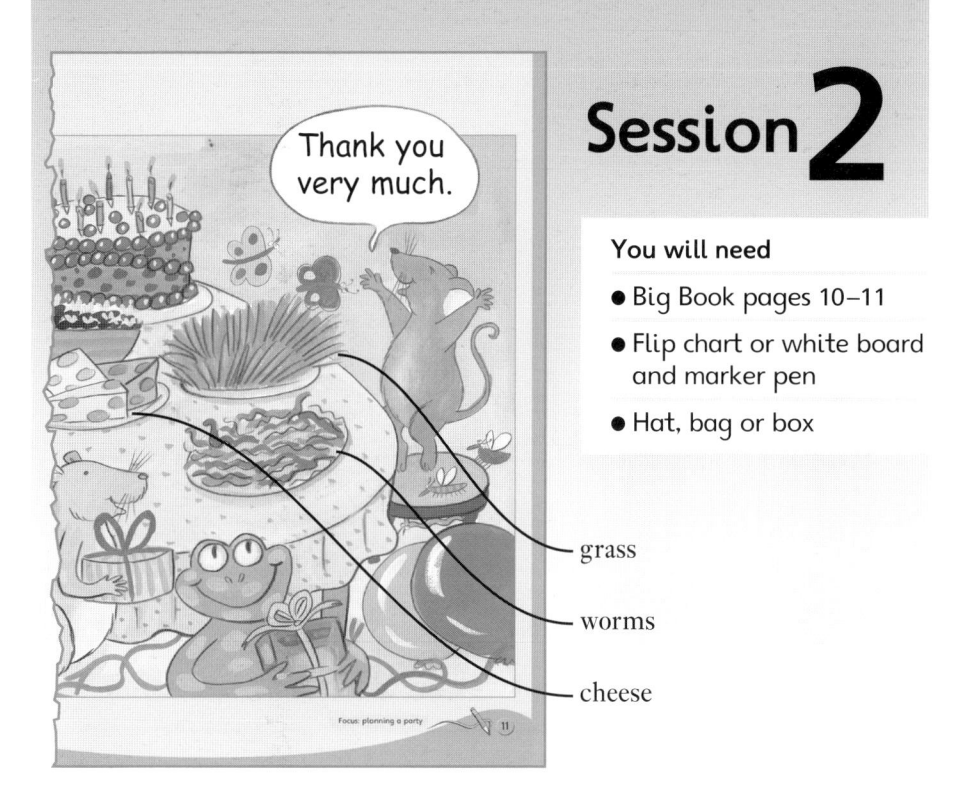

UNIT 3
Max has a party

Making a plan

Teacher scribing

- Ask the children if any of them is going to have a birthday soon. Will they have a party? Ask the class to help to plan a pretend party.

- Look at the picture on Big Book pages 10–11 and ask the children to think about what Max had to do before his party. Scribe their suggestions under a 'Things to do' list on the flip chart.

> Max has invited all his friends. We'll need to do that too, so I'll write, 'Make a list of all my friends' on my 'Things to do' list. We'll need to let them know the day and the time, so I'd better write some invitations. What else has Max done that we'll need to do? Yes, he's made lots of food and organised games to play, so we'll add those to the list.

Group work

- Ask the children to make a list of forfeits as party games, e.g. count from number ten backwards, clap your hands behind your back, hop round a table. (Adult help required.)

Rounding up

- Play 'forfeits' using the suggestions from the group work. Place the forfeits in a hat, bag or box and invite individual children to come out, take a forfeit and perform the instruction.

UNIT 3
Max has a party

Session 3

You will need

- Big Book page 12
- Copies of PCM 5
- Acetate sheet and marker pen

example of completed invitation

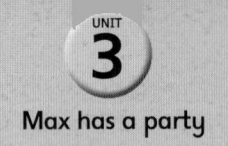

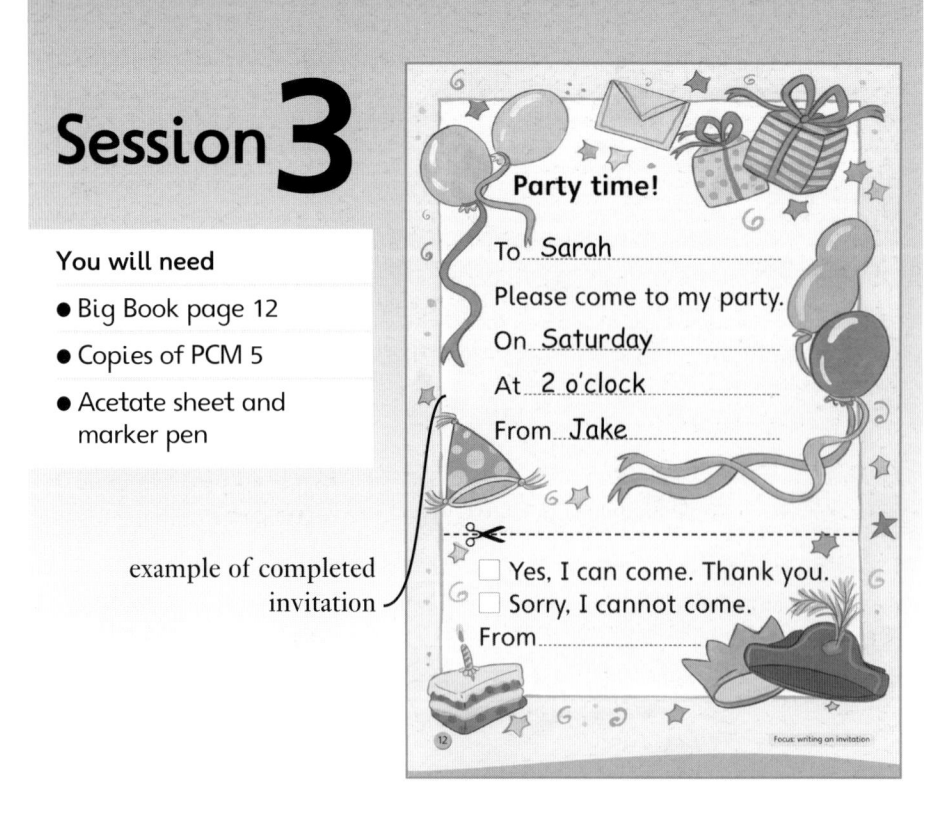

Party time!

To Sarah
Please come to my party.
On Saturday
At 2 o'clock
From Jake

☐ Yes, I can come. Thank you.
☐ Sorry, I cannot come.
From

Shared writing

Teacher demonstration

- Show the class the blank invitation on page 12 of the Big Book.
- Read the text on the frame to the class and ask the children to help you fill the invitation in.

> *What do we need to write first? Yes, we need to write a name next to 'To'. What else do we need to write? That's right, what day it is and what time it is.*

- Go through the information and add it to the frame.
- Explain that you will need to know who's coming, so there's a reply slip on the invitation.

Group work

- PCM 5 This is identical to the invitation on page 12 of the Big Book. Point to the Big Book frame and explain to the children that they will need to complete the invitation.
- Tell them to work with a partner and to discuss what they are going to do before they write anything. When they are sure they know what to do they should complete the invitation.

Rounding up

- Show the class the invitation in the Big Book again and ask them who sent the invitation. How do they know? What important information did they have to write on the invitation? What did the person replying have to do? What did they do if they could not come to the party?

Session 4

UNIT 3 — Max has a party

DON'T FORGET
Party food
 jelly
 cake
 sandwiches

Party games
 Pass the Parcel
 Musical Chairs

list of food and games for the party

You will need
- Big Book page 13
- Copies of PCM 6
- Acetate sheet and marker pen
- Children's white boards and pens

Shared writing

Teacher scribing
- Show the children Big Book page 13. Explain that before you can have the party you need to make a list of the food for the party and the games that you will play.
- Ask the class to suggest what food they like to eat at parties. Point to the illustrations around the frame and ask the children what they would choose for their party.
- Write their suggestions on the acetate sheet, talking through the writing process as you write.
- Ask the children what games they like to play. Remind them of the following: 'Pass the Parcel', 'Dead Lions', 'Musical Chairs', 'The Okey Cokey' and 'Musical Statues'. Write the names of these games on the acetate sheet.

Supported composition
- Show the children the list of food you have written in the Big Book.
- Ask the children to work with a partner, taking it in turns to write on their white boards two items of food that they would like to eat, e.g. 'I like to eat jelly and cake.' Collect in the suggestions and decide which is the most popular food.

Group work
- PCM 6 Tell the children to draw and colour three foods they would like to eat at their party and to write underneath each picture the sentence: 'I like to eat (name of food) at my party.' They can use the labels on the PCM to help with the spellings. Less confident writers may need the words written in highlighter pen for them to write over.

Rounding up
- Ask the children to make a circle and sing 'The Okey Cokey' with them.

STORYWORLDS

Use this unit in conjunction with these stories:
Max and the cat
Max and the apples
Max and the drum
Max wants to fly

DISCOVERY WORLD
Time for a Party (recount)

Name _____

Party time

Write a party invitation.

Party time!

To _____

Please come to my party.

On _____

At _____

From _____

- ☐ Yes, I can come. Thank you.
- ☐ Sorry, I cannot come.

From _____

Unit 3 Max has a party (Session 3) • Skill: writing an invitation
Ask the children to complete the party invitation.

Name _____

PCM 6

Party food

Write about the food you like to eat and draw pictures.

I like to eat _____ at my party.

sandwiches

crisps

cake

samosas

bagels

grapes

biscuits

cheese on sticks

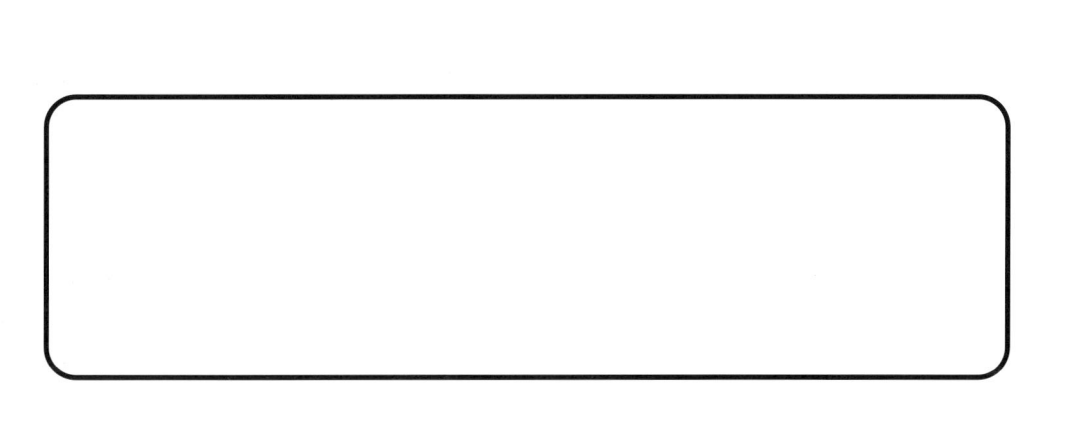

Unit 3 Max has a party (Session 4) • Skill: writing captions for pictures
Ask the children to draw pictures of three foods they would like to eat at their party and to write 'I like to eat (name the food) at my party' under each picture.

UNIT 4

Dragons
Poem with patterned language

Introduction

In this unit, children read a poem by Judith Nicholls about dragons. They then attempt to write their own poem about dragons.

Linked text:
'The big snowball' (Big Book).

TARGET
- use language and structures from reading

PUPIL TARGET
- I can write my own poem

OUTCOME
- poems about dragons

NLS OBJECTIVES
Y1 T2 T11 to learn and recite simple poems and rhymes, with actions, and to re-read them from the text

Y1 T2 T13 to substitute and extend patterns through language play

SCOTTISH 5–14 GUIDELINES
- Imaginative writing
- Spelling
- Handwriting and presentation

Session 1

You will need
- Big Book pages 14–15
- 10 word cards as follows: wood, oak, cave, moss, stone, egg, crack, flame, fire, dragon.

check that the children are familiar with vocabulary

Dragons
Dragonbirth

In the midnight (mists)
of long ago
on a far-off mountainside
there stood
a wild (oak) wood...

In the wild, wet wood
there grew an oak;
beneath the oak
there slept a cave
and in that cave
the (mosses) crept.

Talk for writing

- Talk to the class about dragons. Has anyone read any stories about dragons? Can they remember what dragons are like? Explain that dragons are mythical creatures who are supposed to be able to breathe fire and who hatch from eggs, like reptiles.

- Read the poem on pages 14–15 of the Big Book and check that the children are familiar with all the vocabulary of the poem, e.g. 'mists', 'oak', 'moss'. Read the poem again, stressing the rhythm and encourage the children to join in if they can remember any of the words.

- Point out how the words of the poem are repeated at the end of the lines.

- Tell the children that you are all going to imagine going on a journey to find the dragon's egg. Talk through the poem as you read it again and ask the children to describe the scenes.

> Now we're in the wild, wet, wood, the water is dripping from the trees. Now we've reached the oak tree. Reach out and feel its rough and damp bark.

Group work

- Ask the children to draw a picture of what they think the dragon might look like, e.g. friendly, scary, big, small. Some children may like to write a sentence to describe their dragon.

Rounding up

- Give out the word cards to pairs of children. Re-read the poem and tell the children to arrange themselves in the order of the poem, 'wood', 'oak', 'cave', etc. When you read the poem again they should call out their words in turn.

Session 2

Dragons

> Beneath the moss
> there lay a (stone),
> beneath the (stone)
> there lay an (egg),
> and in that (egg)
> there was a crack.
> From that crack
> there breathed a flame;
> from that flame
> there burst a fire,
> and from that fire
>
> *dragon* came.
>
> by Judith Nicholls

poet repeats words at ends of lines

You will need
- Big Book pages 14–15
- Flip chart or white board and marker pen

Shared writing

Teacher scribing

- Re-read the poem on pages 14–15 of the Big Book, emphasising the rhythm and encouraging the children to join in.

- Tell the children that they are going to help you to write a poem like the dragon poem. It is going to be about finding a dragon's egg. Remind the children about how the poet repeated words at the end of the lines and explain that you will do the same.

- Start the children off by suggesting the first line, and then scribe their suggestions. As you write, show the children how to refine the poem, concentrating on the repeated words and rhythm.

> In the dark, dark room
> there was a door,
> behind the door
> there was a shelf
> and on that shelf
> there sat a box…

Group work

- Ask the children to either continue the poem that you have started in the shared session, or to write one of their own. Some children could copy the verse from the shared session.

Rounding up

- Ask the children to read out the poems they have written during the group work.

Unit 4 Dragons

Session 3

You will need

- Big Book page 16
- Large letter cards as follows: d r a g o n
- Copies of PCM 7
- Flip chart or white board and marker pen

Big Bad Dragon

- green, feathered wings
- angry, white eyes
- sharp, white teeth
- brown, scaly skin

Shared writing

Teacher scribing

- Ask the children to look at the picture of Big Bad Dragon on page 16 of the Big Book. Big Bad Dragon lives in Creepy Castle in Wild Wood and he causes a lot of trouble for the two little dragons Nesta and Ned and their grandma.

- Tell the children that you are going to describe Big Bad Dragon in order to write a poem about him. Ask the children to think of words to describe him. Write their suggestions on the flip chart. Where possible use a colour as part of the description, as this will help to structure the poem.

> How could we describe his eyes? Yes, I could write, 'angry, white eyes'. What about his teeth? Yes, I will write, 'sharp, white teeth'. What colour are his wings? 'Green, feathered wings.' How might we describe his skin? 'Brown, scaly skin.'

Group work

- PCM 7 Ask the children to draw a picture of Big Bad Dragon and to write a character description.

Rounding up

- Give out the letter cards to six children. Re-read the descriptions written in the shared session about Big Bad Dragon. After each phrase, tell the six children to read out their letters in turn, saying the letter names. When they have spelled the word the whole class should say, "dragon". Encourage them to say it in a whisper at first and to get gradually louder.

Session 4

> Dragon
> Five sharp, white teeth.
> Four brown, scaly legs.
> Three yellow tongues of fire.
> Two green, feathered wings.
> One thick, brown tail.
> Dragon

— descriptive poem

You will need
- Big Book pages 16–17
- Copies of PCM 8
- Acetate sheet and marker pen
- Flip chart sheet from Session 3

UNIT 4 — Dragons

Shared writing

Teacher scribing

- Look at the Big Book pages 16–17. Remind the children of the description of Big Bad Dragon. Explain that you are going to write a poem based on their descriptions.

> We're going to write a poem using the descriptions from our brainstorm, but I'm also going to write numbers for each line. I'm going to start with the word 'Dragon', which I'm going to write on a line of its own. Then my next line will be 'Five'. What could Big Bad Dragon have five of? Yes, I could describe his teeth, 'Five sharp, white teeth'. Four? Now what could we write to go with that? 'Four brown, scaly legs'.

- Complete the poem, using appropriate descriptions, e.g. 'Three yellow tongues of fire', 'Two green, feathered wings', 'One thick, brown tail'.
- At the end of the poem repeat the word 'Dragon'.
- As you write, draw attention to phonics and spelling features that are appropriate to the children's suggestions, for example, CVC words.

Group work

- PCM 8 Ask the children to write their own poem about Big Bad Dragon. Some children may like to work on the poem developed during the shared session.

Rounding up

- Select 15 children and divide them into groups of five, four, three, two and one. Ask them to look at the poem on page 17 and to read the line that matches their number. The group of five should read, "Five sharp, white teeth", etc. The rest of the class should whisper the word "dragon" between each line.
- Alternatively, share the work on the children's poems.

STORYWORLDS

Use this unit in conjunction with these stories:
The big snowball
The bag of coal
Creepy Castle
Fire in Wild Wood

Name _____

What is Big Bad Dragon like?

Draw a picture of Big Bad Dragon and describe him.

He has _____ eyes.

He has _____ teeth.

_____ wings.

_____.

Unit 4 Dragons (Session 3) • Skill: writing a description
Ask the children to draw a picture of Big Bad Dragon and to complete the sentences describing him.

Name _____

Dragon poem

Write a poem about Big Bad Dragon.

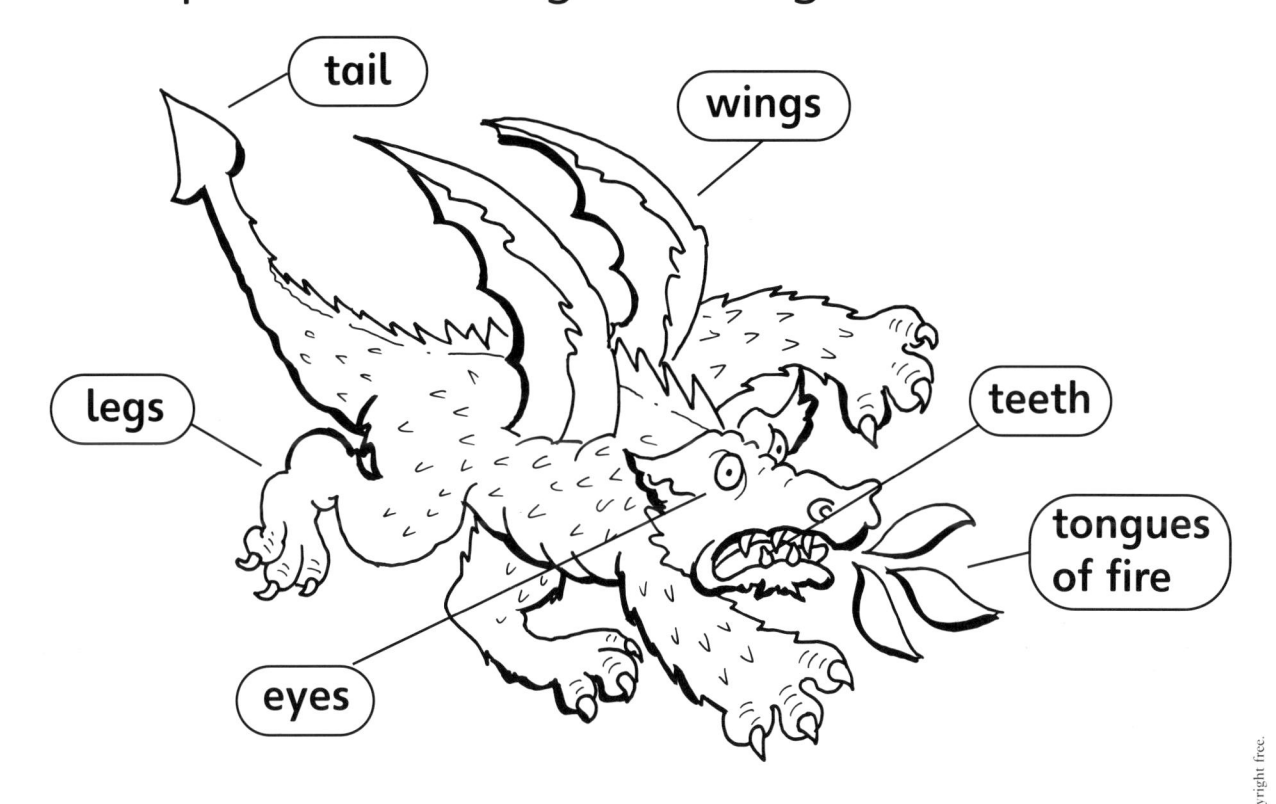

- tail
- wings
- legs
- teeth
- tongues of fire
- eyes

Five _____

Four _____

Three _____

Two _____

One _____

DRAGON

Unit 4 Dragons (Session 4) • **Skill:** writing a poem
Ask the children to write their own poem about Big Bad Dragon.
Alternatively, they can work on the poem developed during the shared session.

UNIT 5

The Wolf and the Kids
Traditional story

Introduction
In this unit, children recall the sequence of a plot and use it as a model for writing a story.

Linked text:
'The Wolf and the Kids' (Big Book).

TARGET
- write a story that can be re-read

PUPIL TARGET
- I can re-tell a story plot

OUTCOME
- a re-telling of a story

NLS OBJECTIVES

Y1 T2 T10   to identify and compare basic story elements

Y1 T2 T16   to use some of the elements of known stories to structure own writing

Y1 T2 S5   to continue demarcating sentences in writing, ending a sentence with a full stop

SCOTTISH 5–14 GUIDELINES
- Imaginative writing
- Punctuation and structure

Session 1

You will need
- Big Book pages 18–20

examples of speech for speech bubbles:
Mother Goat: Don't open the door.
wolf: I am your mother.

Talk for writing

- Ask the class if anyone knows the story of 'The Wolf and the Kids'. Check that everyone knows 'kids' is the word for young goats.

- Look at the six pictures on pages 18, 19 & 20 of the Big Book. These pictures show the main events of the story about the wolf and the kids. Give a lively retelling of the story, using the pictures as prompts. (Mother Goat goes out and warns the kids not to let the wolf into the house. The wolf claims to be Mother Goat, but the kids spot his black feet. The wolf dips his feet in flour and the kids open the door to him. The wolf captures the kids in his sack. Mother Goat returns and chases the wolf.)

Group work

- Encourage the children to role-play the story with adult help. The adult should be the narrator and two confident children should be the wolf and Mother Goat. The rest of the group should be the kids. Start the story "Once upon a time …"

Rounding up

- Encourage the children to retell the story in their own words. Keep the pace of the retelling by asking the children what happened next at each stage of the story.

Session 2

UNIT 5 — The Wolf and the Kids

You will need
- Big Book pages 18–20
- Circular pieces of card for speech bubbles and Blu-Tack

examples of speech for speech bubbles:
wolf: Open up kids.
the kids: Help!

Shared writing

Teacher demonstration

- Look again at the six pictures and discuss with the children what the characters might say in each picture. For example, Mother Goat might say, "Don't open the door." Talk through all the pictures, deciding on suitable speech.

- Model writing the speech bubbles for the class, talking through the writing process. Think aloud to share with the children the decisions you are making about your writing. Talk specifically about full stops to demarcate sentences and capital letters to start each sentence.

   > In this first picture Mother Goat is going out, so I am going to write, 'Don't open the door.'

- When you have written the speech bubble, ask a child to stick it next to the correct picture. Re-read the speech bubble with the class.

- Continue to write speech bubbles for each picture.

Group work

- Give each child a speech bubble, and ask the children to discuss who spoke the words. The children should then read the words in the style of the character. (Adult help required.)

Rounding up

- Play 'What's the time, Mr Wolf?' You take the part of the wolf and stand with your back to the class. They stand as far back from you as they can. In order to step closer to you, they must copy the description you give them. For example, you say, "blood-red eyes" and they must echo, "blood-red eyes" and take a step nearer you. At suitable moments you choose to describe yourself and then turn to chase after the children. For example, "I've got rows of sharp teeth for eating with." At this point run after the children and try to 'catch' one or two.

Session 3

You will need
- Big Book page 21
- Copies of PCM 9
- Acetate sheet and marker pen

Shared writing/Making a plan

- Tell the children that you are going to write a story plan for the story of 'The Wolf and the Kids'. Look at the first two headings on the story frame on page 21 of the Big Book ('Characters' and 'Setting'). Explain to the children what these headings mean. Talk with the children about the characters in the story and list them under the heading. Then talk about the setting of the story – Mother Goat's house.

- Point out the other headings ('Beginning', 'Middle' and 'End') and help the children to map the events of the story under these headings.

> Now what happened at the beginning of the story? Yes, that's right, Mother Goat went out leaving the kids at home. What happened next? Yes, the wolf knocked on the door.

- Continue mapping the story on the plan.

Group work

- PCM 9 Ask the children to write captions to go with each section of the story.

Rounding up

- Talk about good phrases with which to start and finish a traditional story.

Session 4

UNIT 5 — The Wolf and the Kids

Story plot

Characters
Mother Goat, wolf, kids

Setting
Mother Goat's house

Beginning
Mother Goat went out, leaving the kids at home.

Middle
The wolf came to the house.

End

example of story plan

You will need

- Big Book pages 18–19
- 12 word cards: The wolf looked for the kids under table in clock up chimney (and full stop card)
- Copies of PCM 10
- Flip chart or white board and marker pen

Shared writing

Teacher demonstration

- Explain to the children that you are going to write the middle of the story, when the wolf bursts into the house and captures the kids.
- Orally re-tell the story up to that point, using the pictures on pages 18–19 of the Big Book to prompt the talk.
- On the flip chart, start to write the story from this middle point, talking through the writing process as you write.

> It's not the beginning of the story, so I don't need a story opener. I can just begin, 'As soon as the door was opened the wolf burst in. He began to look for the kids. He found the first kid hiding behind the door.'

- Continue writing the middle section of the story, up to the return of Mother Goat.

Group work

- PCM 10 This is a frame for the children to write the part of the story when the wolf bursts into Mother Goat's house and captures the kids in his sack.

Rounding up

- Tell the children to work with a partner. Give out a word card to each pair. Dictate a sentence to the class, e.g.

> The wolf looked for the kids. The wolf looked under the table. The wolf looked in the clock. The wolf looked up the chimney.

- Those children who hold a word card from that sentence should come out and line themselves up in sentence order (including the full stop). When they are happy that they have made the sentence they should read it out with each pair saying their word in turn and the full stop coming at the end.

Use this unit in conjunction with these stories:
The Wolf and the Kids
The Ugly Duckling
The Lake of Stars
The Straw House

Name

The Wolf and the Kids

Write captions for the pictures.

Beginning

Middle

End

Name

What did the wolf do?

Write the story.

- wolf
- kids
- chimney

- table
- door
- sack

As soon as the kids opened the door the wolf burst in.

He began to _____

Unit 5 The Wolf and the Kids (Session 4) • Skill: writing the 'middle section' of a story
Ask the children to write the part of the story when the wolf bursts into Mother Goat's house and captures the kids in his sack.

UNIT 6

Dolphins
Non-chronological report

Introduction
In this unit, children study photographs to learn about dolphins and develop these facts into a non-chronological report.

Linked text:
'Dipper to the rescue' (Big Book).

TARGET
- use words appropriate to different text forms

PUPIL TARGET
- I can write a report about dolphins

OUTCOME
- a report about dolphins

NLS OBJECTIVES

Y1 T2 T22	to write labels for diagrams
Y1 T2 T24	to write simple questions
Y1 T2 T25	to write simple non-chronological reports
Y1 T2 S6	to use the term *sentence* appropriately

SCOTTISH 5–14 GUIDELINES
- Functional writing
- Handwriting and presentation
- Punctuation and structure

Session 1

You will need
- Big Book pages 22–23
- Children's white boards and pens
- Copies of PCM 11
- Flip chart or white board and marker pen

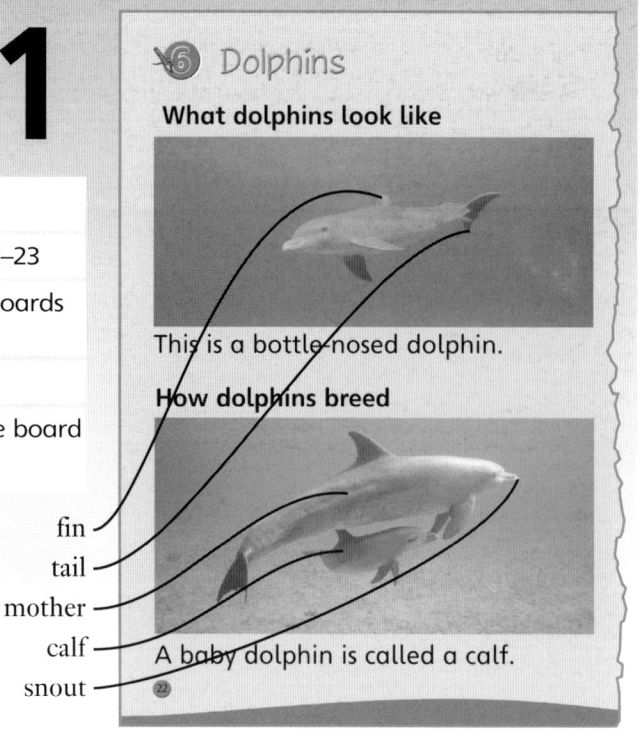

Dolphins
What dolphins look like

This is a bottle-nosed dolphin.

How dolphins breed

fin
tail
mother
calf
snout

A baby dolphin is called a calf.

Talk for writing
- Look at the pictures on pages 22–23 of the Big Book. Ask the children if they know anything about dolphins. Have they ever been to an underwater world and seen dolphins? Introduce the concept that dolphins are mammals and not fish.

Making a plan
- Make a chart on the flip chart with the headings, 'What I know' and 'What I want to know'. Write the information that children already know about dolphins in the first column.
- Write the following 'question' words on the flip chart: 'What', 'Where', 'How'. Help the children to formulate questions for the second column. Demonstrate the use of a question mark at the end of a question.

Shared writing
Supported composition
- Tell the children to work with a partner and to write on their white boards one question about dolphins to which they would like to know the answer. They should start their question with one of the question words. Help those children who need further guidance.
- Write some of the children's questions on the 'What I want to know' section of the chart.

Group work
- PCM 11 Ask the children to complete the columns in the chart. (Adult help required.)

Rounding up
- Ask the children to share a question with the class, scribe this on the flip chart and read it together. Prompt the children to suggest the correct punctuation for a question.

UNIT 6 Dolphins

Session 2

You will need
- Big Book pages 22–23
- Yes/No cards for each pair of children
- Copies of PCM 11 from Session 1
- Acetate sheet and marker pen

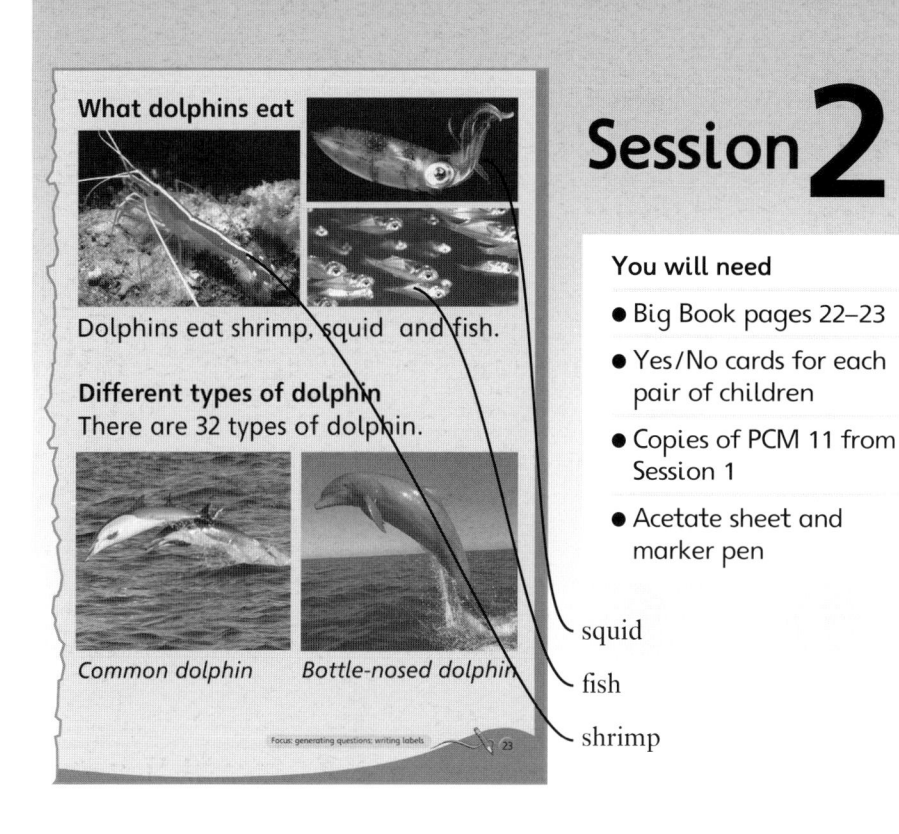

Talk for writing

- Remind the children about the questions they asked about dolphins. Look again at the pictures on pages 22–23 of the Big Book. Discuss the detail in each picture, e.g. point out the fin and the tail. Do the same with all the pictures, including the following details: mother, calf, mammal, squid, fish, shrimp.

Shared writing

Teacher demonstration

- Tell the children that you are going to write some labels for the pictures. Remind them that labels identify a particular feature. Talk through the writing process as you write the labels.
- Include relevant word level work, e.g.

> Who knows what letter I need to write first for the word 'tail'?

Group work

- PCM 11 Ensure that the children have their own copies of PCM 11 from Session 1. Ask the children to complete the sentences at the bottom of the page.

Rounding up

- Give out the 'Yes'/'No' cards to pairs of children. Tell them you are going to say some facts about dolphins and they are to decide if the facts are true or not. If the facts are true, they should hold up their 'Yes' cards and if they are not true they should hold up their 'No' cards, e.g.

> Dolphins are mammals. Dolphins are fish. Dolphins live on land. Dolphins live in the sea. A baby dolphin is called a calf. A baby dolphin is called a cub.

Unit 6 Dolphins

Session 3

You will need

- Big Book pages 22–23
- Flip chart or white board and marker pen
- Word cards as follows: fin, snout, tail, calf, fish, shrimp, squid, mother, mammal

Dolphin report

- Introduction
  Dolphins are mammals that live in the sea.
- What dolphins look like

- How dolphins breed

Shared writing

Teacher demonstration

- Tell the children that you are going to write some notes about dolphins which will be helpful when you come to write a report in the next session. Explain that notes are the most important bits of information which remind you of what you want to write about.

- Talk through the writing process as you make the notes on the flip chart.

  > I'm going to put 'Dolphins' as a heading. First of all I'm going to describe what they look like, so I'll put a sub-heading, 'What dolphins look like'.

- Give the children two minutes to discuss with a partner what they know about the appearance of dolphins and then take in some of their answers. Shape their answers into suitable words for bullet points under the headings.

  > Yes, you're right, dolphins have fins. Now as I'm only writing notes all I'm going to write is the word 'fins'.

- Continue until you have information under each of the headings, 'What dolphins look like', 'How dolphins breed', 'What dolphins eat', 'Different types of dolphin'.

Group work

- Ask the children to draw a picture of a mother dolphin with her calf. They should then label the picture, e.g. tail, fin, snout, calf.

Rounding up

- Give out the word cards to pairs of children. Tell them that you are going to choose a sub-heading and if they think they have a card that could make a bullet point under that heading then they should stand up. For example, when you call out the heading 'How dolphins breed' the children with the word cards for 'mammal', 'mother' and 'calf' should stand up. Do the same with the other headings.

Session 4

UNIT 6 — Dolphins

- What dolphins eat
- Different types of dolphin

Simple, non-chronological report

You will need
- Big Book pages 24–25
- Notes from Session 3
- Copies of PCM 12
- Acetate sheet and marker pen

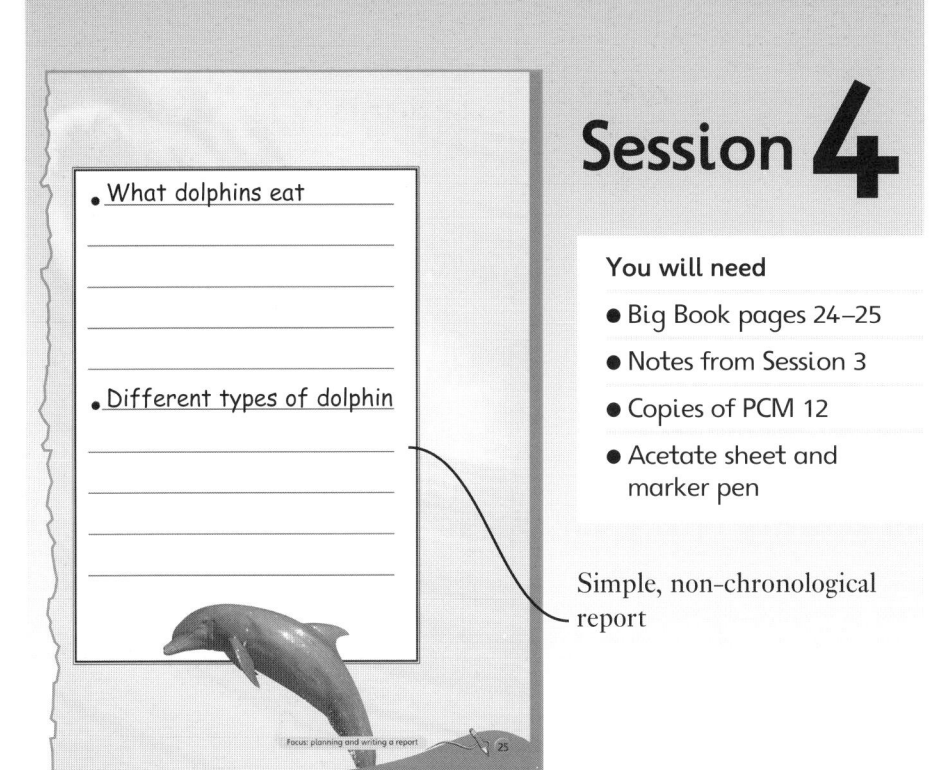

Talk for writing

- Tell the children that you are going to write a report on dolphins based on your notes from the previous session. Explain that a report tells things as they are and does not include what people think about things. So a story about a dolphin might talk about the dolphin being happy or sad, but a report about dolphins contains just the facts.

Shared writing

Teacher demonstration

- Look at the report frame on pages 24–25 of the Big Book.

> Today we are writing a report about dolphins, so the heading says, 'Dolphin report'. Now what did we write in our notes? We listed the facts. Now, dolphins live in the sea but are they fish? No, they are mammals and that is going to be the first fact for my report. I am writing in sentences, not just listing words as we did in our notes, so for the introduction I'm going to write, 'Dolphins are mammals that live in the sea.'

- Continue modelling the report, giving facts under the relevant headings. Re-read the information as you write it.

Group work

- **PCM 12** Ask the children to complete the report on dolphins.

Rounding up

- Ask two or three individual children to read out their reports. Ask the class if they think that they have included all the information in their reports, or whether there is anything else to add.

STORYWORLDS

Use this unit in conjunction with these stories:
- Dipper to the rescue
- Dipper gets stuck
- Dipper in danger
- Dipper and the old wreck

DISCOVERY WORLD
- Eyes
- Materials
- Amazing Eggs
- What's Underneath?
(all reports)

Name _____

Dolphin facts

Fill in the boxes and complete the sentences.

What I know	What I want to know

❶ Dolphins are _____

❷ A baby dolphin is called a _____

❸ A dolphin has a long nose called a _____

❹ Dolphins eat _____ and _____

mammals   calf   fish   snout   shrimp

Unit 6 Dolphins (Sessions 1 and 2) • Skill: writing facts
Ask the children to complete the columns in the chart. (Adult help required.)
In the next session, ask the children to complete the sentences at the bottom of the page using the words in the box.

Name _____

Dolphin report

Write a report on dolphins.

Introduction

Dolphins are mammals that live in the sea.

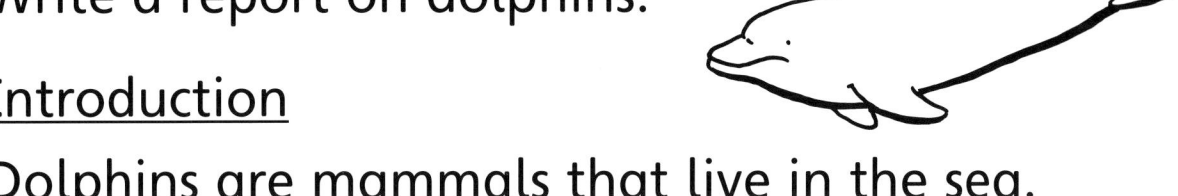

What dolphins look like

How dolphins breed

What dolphins eat

Different types of dolphin

UNIT 7

Pet poems
Poems on similar themes

Introduction
In this unit, children write simple poems based on a repetitive model.

Linked text:
'Harry's elephant' (Big Book).

TARGET
- write a poem

PUPIL TARGET
- I can write a poem from a model

OUTCOME
- class and individual poems about pets

NLS OBJECTIVES

Y1 T3 T15	to use poems as models for own writing
Y1 T3 T16	to compose own poetic sentences using repetitive patterns
Y1 T3 S6	to reinforce knowledge of term *sentence*
Y1 T3 W7	to spell common irregular words

SCOTTISH 5–14 GUIDELINES
- Functional writing
- Personal writing
- Imaginative writing
- Spelling
- Handwriting and presentation

Session 1

You will need
- Flip chart or white board and marker pen

rhyming words to cover up

Pet poems

I want...
Richard owns a rabbit
Chloe's got a cat
Tricia has a terrapin
But me?
I want a *rat!*

Barry loves his budgie
Donna walks her dog
Parma rides his pony
But me?
I want a *frog!*

Talk for writing

- Ask the children to tell you what pets they have at home. What do they have to do for their pets? What do their pets like to eat?
- Ask them if they think all animals make good pets. Would an elephant make a good pet? Why not?
- Suggest some different pets and ask the children to put up their hand if they think the animal would make a good pet, e.g. lion, cat, kangaroo, goldfish, monkey, seal, mouse, bear, frog. Ask them to explain why they think the animal would make a good pet.

Shared writing

Teacher demonstration
- Tell the children that you are going to write a list of all the pets the children have or would like to have. Write the word 'dog' on the flip chart and ask individual children to sound out the three phonemes in the word. Ask the children to put up their hands if a dog would be their favourite pet.
- Ask for other pets and help the children to sound out the phonemes in the words, e.g. fish, cat, rabbit, bird, pony.

Group work
- Tell the children to work with a partner and to write down a pet they either have or would like to have. They should discuss how to spell the word before they write it. Tell them to discuss and write a sentence with their partner to say if the animal would make a good pet or not.

Rounding up
- Ask individual children to read out their sentences about their pet.

Session 2

UNIT 7 — Pet poems

> Harry holds his hamster
> Pauline's pigeons coo
> Gerry feeds his gerbils
> But me?
> I want a zoo!
>
> *by Wes Magee*

name of pet owner and pet start with the same letter

You will need
- Big Book pages 26–27
- Post-it notes
- Copies of PCM 13
- Flip chart or white board and pen

Talk for writing

- Show the class the Big Book pages 26–27 and read the poem aloud. Encourage the children to follow the words as you read.
- Ask the children if the child in the poem wants a good pet. What pet do they think she would choose from the zoo? Do they think her parents will let her keep any of her pets?

Shared writing

Teacher scribing

- Cover the rhyming words with Post-it notes and read the poem again asking the children to tell you the missing words.
- Ask the children to suggest names from the class that could go in the poem. Point out that the name of the pet owner and the pet start with the same letter, e.g. 'Richard owns a rabbit'. Ask the chosen children to write their names on a Post-it note and place these over the names in the poem.
- Tell the children that you are going to write a list of different animals on the flip chart and that they must help you to think of a name which has the same starting letter, e.g. 'Angela has an ant, Ben has a bear', etc.
- Ask the class to read the poem with you again.

Group work

- PCM 13 This is a poetry frame. Ask the children to complete the poem.

Rounding up

- Ask the children to share with the class their poems from the group work.

UNIT 7
Pet poems

Session 3

You will need
- Big Book page 28
- Acetate sheet and marker pen

examples of descriptive alliterative words

Poetry brainstorm

- bear — brown, beautiful, black
- lizard — lively, laughing
- cat — clever, cool, cuddly
- dog — dancing, delightful, dizzy
- frog — funny, fantastic, friendly

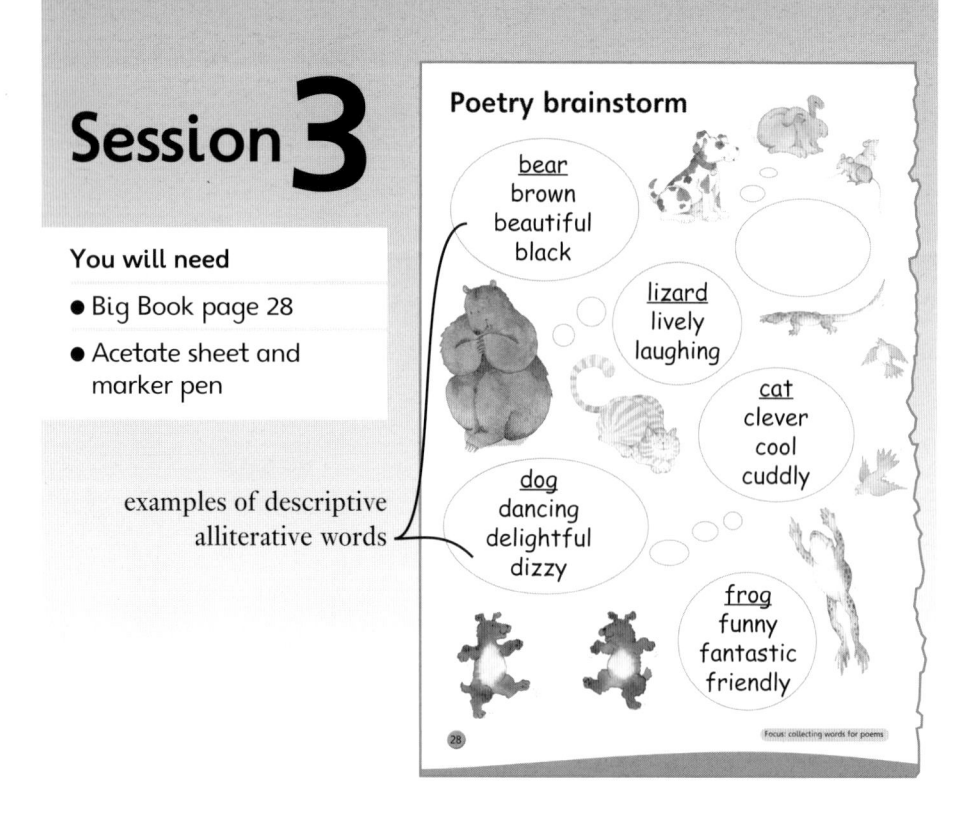

Shared writing

Teacher scribing

- Explain to the class that they are going to write their own poems about pets, but that first you want them to help you to think of exciting words to describe the pets they might choose. Use the 'poetry brainstorm' picture on page 28 of the Big Book.

- Ask them to suggest alliterative words that might describe a cat. Write the word 'cat' on the brainstorm web and all the words that link with it, such as 'clever', 'cuddly', 'cool', 'cold', 'cunning'. Emphasise the sound of the letter 'c' and talk through the writing process as you write.

- Continue to brainstorm other animals, e.g. 'bear' ('brown', 'big', 'beautiful', 'black'), 'dog' ('dancing', 'delightful', 'dizzy', 'dark'.) Keep the suggestions for the session when the children write their own poems.

Group work

- Ask the children to work with a partner and to think of another animal and write two or three linking words.

Rounding up

- Make up some riddles and ask the children to guess the animal, e.g.

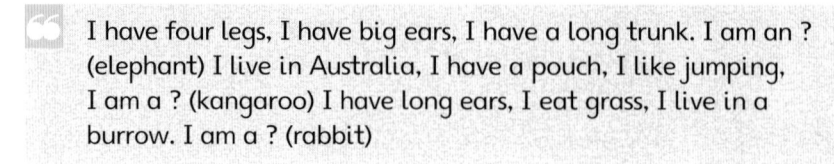

> I have four legs, I have big ears, I have a long trunk. I am an ? (elephant) I live in Australia, I have a pouch, I like jumping, I am a ? (kangaroo) I have long ears, I eat grass, I live in a burrow. I am a ? (rabbit)

Session 4

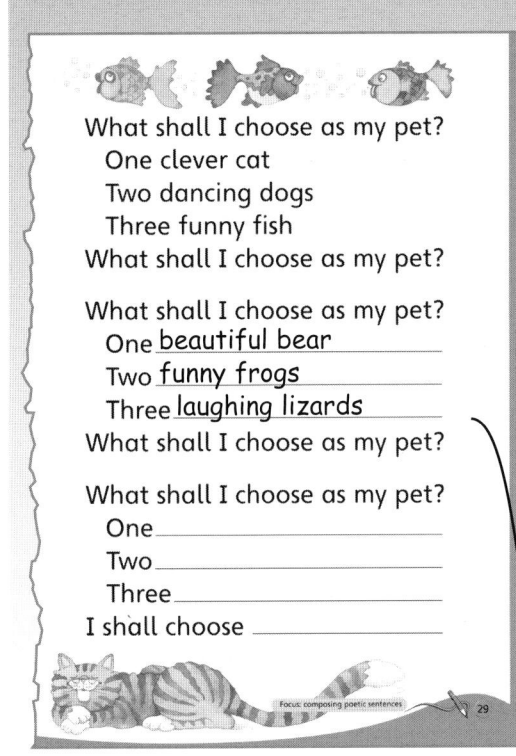

UNIT 7 — Pet poems

> What shall I choose as my pet?
> One clever cat
> Two dancing dogs
> Three funny fish
> What shall I choose as my pet?
>
> What shall I choose as my pet?
> One <u>beautiful bear</u>
> Two <u>funny frogs</u>
> Three <u>laughing lizards</u>
> What shall I choose as my pet?
>
> What shall I choose as my pet?
> One _____
> Two _____
> Three _____
> I shall choose _____

poem using alliterative phrases

You will need

- Big Book pages 28–29
- Acetate sheet and marker pen
- Children's white boards and pens
- Copies of PCM 14
- Acetate sheet from Session 3

Shared writing

Teacher demonstration

- Tell the children that you want them to help you to write a poem.
- Point to the brainstorm suggestions that they made in the last session. Explain that they will need to use words to describe their pet in the poem.
- Read the opening refrain on page 29 of the Big Book, 'What shall I choose as my pet?' Then read the first verse to the class.
- Ask the children to suggest other animals for the second verse using the words from Session 3 and write these on the frame.
- Finally ask for three more suggestions for the last verse and talk through the writing process as you complete the frame.
- End by completing the last line with the pet you like most.

Supported composition

- Tell the children to work with a partner and to write the following: 'One', 'Two', 'Three' down the left hand side of their white boards. Ask them to use the alliterative phrases from Session 3 and to write their own choice of animals.

Group work

- PCM 14 Ask the children to write their own poem. Collect in their verses to make a class poetry book at a later date.

Rounding up

- Share some of the children's own poems and talk about the alliterative words they have used.

STORYWORLDS

Use this unit in conjunction with these stories:

- Harry's elephant
- Harry's snake
- Harry's monkey
- Harry's seal

DISCOVERY WORLD

How to Choose a Pet (report)

Pets

Complete the poem.

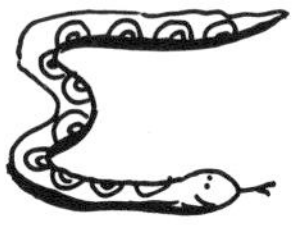

Sally likes her _____

_____ rat

Manjit _____

But I like my _____.

Peter likes his _____

_____ frog

Libby _____

But I like my _____.

Ben likes his _____

_____ snail

Abdul _____

But I like my _____.

Name

What shall I choose as my pet?

Write a poem.

What shall I choose as my pet?

One _____

Two _____

Three _____

What shall I choose as my pet?

What _____ _____ choose _____ _____ _____ ?

One _____

Two _____

Three _____

Unit 7 Pet poems (Session 4) • Skill: writing a poem
Ask the children to write their own poem.

UNIT 8

The country park
Recount and information text

Introduction
In this unit, children look at the map of a country park and then write a simple recount and brochure.

Linked texts:
'Our World' stories, Stage 6.

TARGET
- write a recount
- write statements and label information

PUPIL TARGET
- I can write a recount

OUTCOME
- a simple recount
- a page from a brochure about a country park

NLS OBJECTIVES

Y1 T3 T20	to write simple recounts linked to topics of interest
Y1 T3 T21	to use the language and features of non-fiction texts, e.g. labelled diagrams
Y1 T3 T22	to write own questions
Y1 T3 S5	other common uses of capitalisation
Y1 T3 W1	to identify phonemes in speech and writing

SCOTTISH 5–14 GUIDELINES
- Functional writing
- Spelling
- Handwriting and presentation

Session 1

You will need
- Big Book pages 30–31
- Acetate sheet and marker pen

8 The country park

Car park

Talk for writing

- Ask the children if they have ever been to a country park. What did they do there?
- Show the class the map on pages 30–31 of the Big Book.
- Talk through the things on the map and show them the paths that go to the different parts of the country park.
- Discuss the details of the picture with the children. Look at the animals in the pets corner, what are the young called? Look at the nature trail, what would they see on the trail?
- Ask the children to turn to a partner and discuss what they would like to do in the park. Where would they go first? Where would they eat? What do they think would be the most fun?

UNIT 8
The country park

labels for the country park

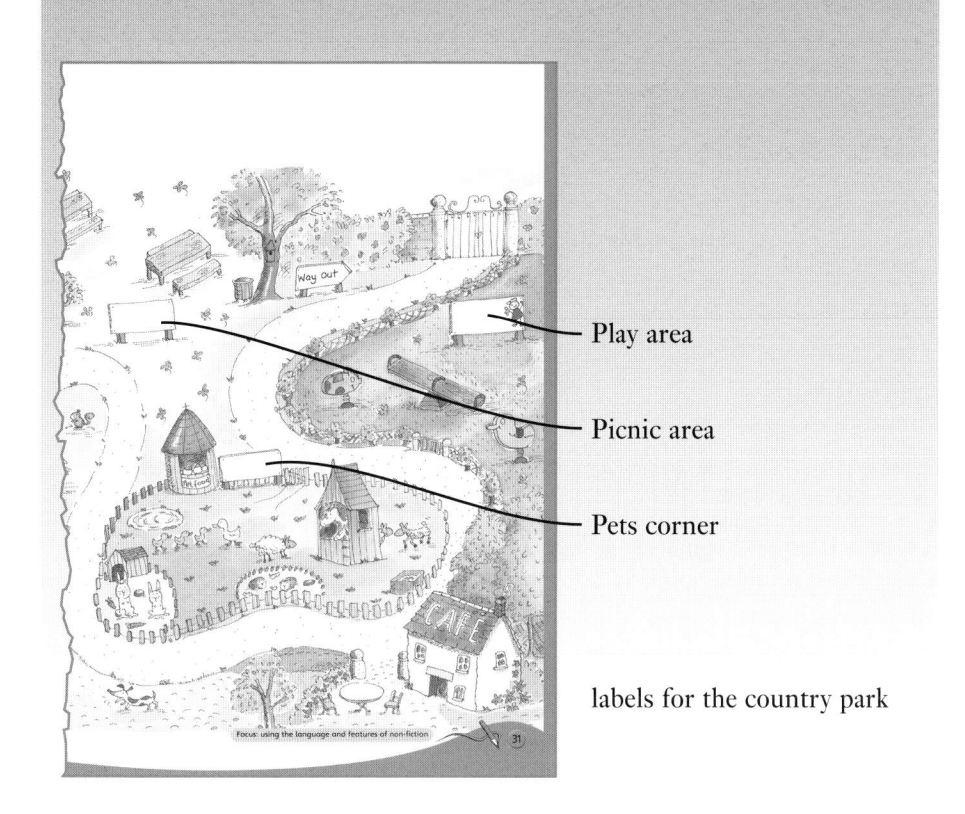

Shared writing

Teacher scribing
- Explain that you need to label the map so that visitors will know where to go.
- Ask the children to suggest things that should be labelled. Write the labels on the blank sign posts and talk through the writing process as you write.
- Pull out links to word level work. For example, ask the children to tell you how many phonemes there are in the following words: park (3), pet (3), trail (4), picnic (6), play (3), pond (4), chick (3), rabbit (5).

Group work
- Ask the children to work in pairs to draw a path through an imaginary country park. They should draw and label the things they might see en route, e.g. trees, animals, bench, etc.

Rounding up
- Discuss with the children the need to label the map of the country park. What might happen if things weren't labelled?

UNIT 8
The country park

Session 2

You will need
- Big Book pages 32–33
- Copies of PCM 15
- Acetate sheet and marker pen

pictures showing account of a visit to the park

Talk for writing

- Show the children Big Book page 32. This shows the route that Amy and Daniel took through the park. Ask the children where Amy and Daniel went first. Then where did they go? Where did they go next? Where have they still got to visit?

Shared writing

Teacher demonstration

- Show the children the recount frame on page 33 and discuss how you are going to write an account of what Amy and Daniel did in the park.
- Ask the children what you should write in the first section.

> That's right. First Amy and Daniel went to the nature trail. What did they see there? Yes, they saw a squirrel.

- Write the sentences on the frame, talking through the writing process as you write.

> The first word in each of my paragraphs should tell us the order that Amy and Daniel did things. What do I need to remember when I write 'Amy' and 'Daniel'? Yes, they are names and they need a capital letter.

- Complete the writing frame encouraging the children to give you contributions.

UNIT 8

The country park

A visit to the park

First _Amy and Daniel went to the nature trail._
Then _they had lunch in the picnic area._
Next _they went to the pets corner and saw a rabbit and a pony._
Finally _Amy and Daniel went to the play area and played on the see-saw._

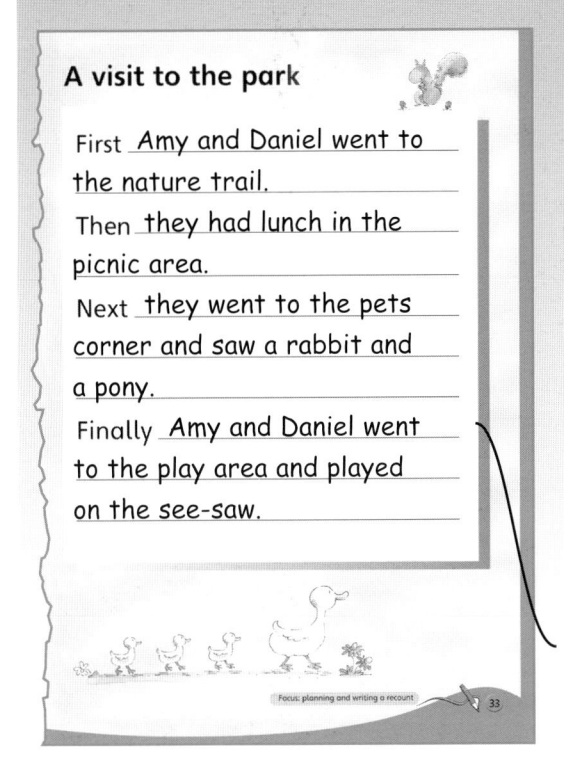

completed recount of the route through the park

Group work

- PCM 15 Ask the children to complete the recount, writing the route that Amy and Daniel took through the country park.

Rounding up

- Ask individual children to read out their recounts from the group work.
- Ask the children how many sentences they wrote. Do they make sense? Have they remembered the punctuation?
- At a later date display the group work on the classroom wall.

UNIT 8

The country park

Session 3

You will need

- Big Book pages 34–35
- Copies of PCM 16
- Acetate sheet and marker pen

example of a country park brochure

A great day out!

Things to do

Pets corner
- Visit the baby animals
- Watch the chicks
- Stroke a baby rabbit

Nature trail
- See a squirrel
- Look at the pond
- Try to spot an owl

Where to eat
-
-
-

Play area
-
-
-

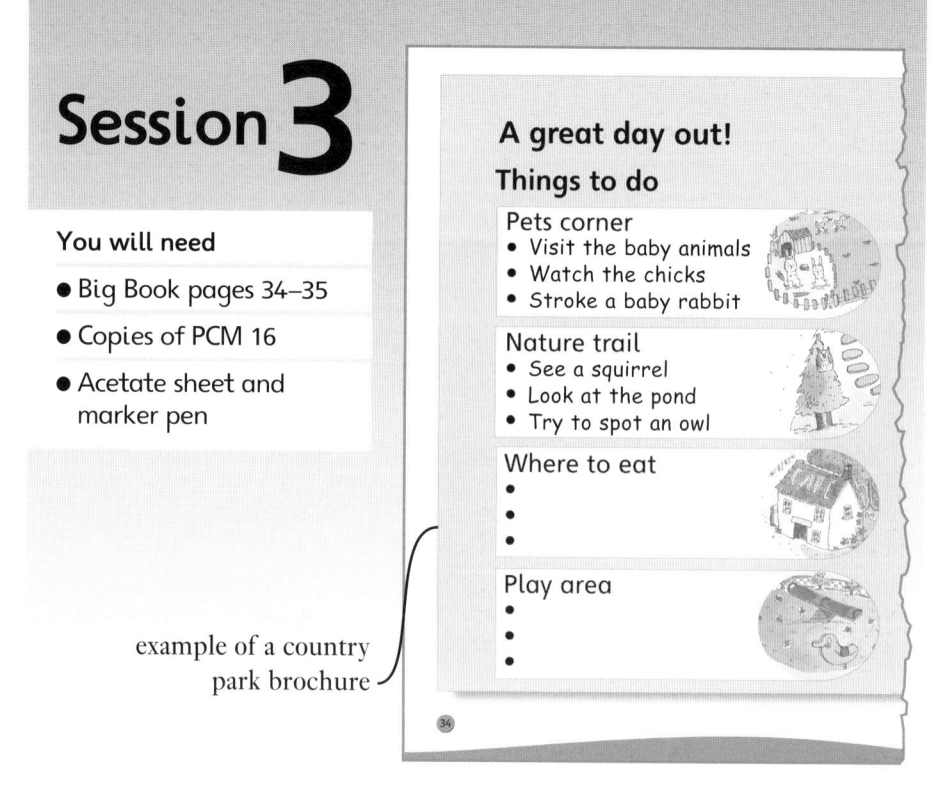

Shared writing

Teacher demonstration/Teacher scribing

- Look at the 'brochure' on pages 34–35 of the Big Book, and explain that it tells people about what they can see and do in the park.

- Read the title of the brochure and ask the children to help you to complete the brochure.

- Point to the first side heading and talk about how the heading helps the reader to find out about the things they want to know. Ask the children what you should write under the heading. Talk about the bullet points and explain that these are to help you to mention all the facts.

> How many things should I write about under 'Pets corner'? Yes, there are three things to mention. What do you think they are? We could put 'Visit the baby animals' and 'Watch the chicks eating their corn', then 'Stroke a baby rabbit'.

- Complete the sections, talking through the writing process and asking the children to help you to spell phonically regular words.

Group work

- PCM 16 Ask the children to complete the sentences about what you can do in the country park. Tell them that they will finish the PCM in a later session.

Rounding up

- Recap some of the non-fiction features of the text with the children, e.g.

> Why are there side headings in the brochure? How do the bullet points help writers?

Session 4

Mayfields Country Park

How to find us

Greenfields
Near Riverside
Forestshire   Tel: 5204
Opening times
Monday–Saturday 10am–5pm
Sunday 11am–4pm

You will need
- Big Book pages 34–35
- Acetate sheet and marker pen
- Completed acetate sheet from Session 3
- Children's copies of PCM 16 from Session 3
- Flip chart
- Brochures from local places of interest (optional)
- completed information text

Talk for writing

- Ask the children to look again at the brochure. Explain that the information about the park is not enough to get people to go to the park. Can they think of any other information the brochure should give? e.g. 'Where is the country park?' 'When does it open?' Write these questions on the flip chart, drawing attention to the question mark at the end of the question.

- Ask the children what they would need to put in the brochure to make sure people could find it, e.g. a map or directions.

- If possible, give the children examples of brochures from local places of interest to compare and stimulate the discussion.

Shared writing

Teacher demonstration

- On page 35 of the Big Book, show the children how to organise the additional information as a page for the brochure.

- Draw a map of how to find the park, compile the address and telephone number and opening times.

Group work

- PCM 16 Ensure that the children have their own copies of the PCM from the previous session and ask them to draw a map and complete the address, telephone number and opening times.

Rounding up

- Ask the children where they would like to go for a great day out. Collect in their suggestions and write them on the flip chart. Ask the children when you should use capital letters, e.g. for place names and the first word.

- Tell the children to vote on where they would like to go, and find out the most popular place.

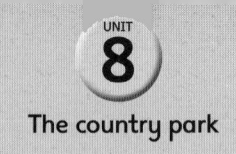

UNIT 8
The country park

STORYWORLDS

Use this unit in conjunction with these stories:
- The school fair
- The big boots
- The lost costume
- The castle

DISCOVERY WORLD

A Closer Look at Parks
(information book)

Maps
(information book)

Name _____

Amy and Daniel at the country park

Complete the sentences. The words in the box will help you.

> First   Next   Then   Finally

nature trail

picnic area

_____ nature trail.

_____ picnic area.

_____ pets corner.

_____ they went to the play area.

pets corner

play area

Unit 8 The country park (Session 2) • **Skill:** completing a recount
Ask the children to complete the recount, writing the route that Amy and Daniel took through the country park.

Name

A country park brochure

Write about the country park.

Mayfields Country Park
A great day out!

You can visit the pets corner.

You _____ the nature trail.

You _____ .

You _____ .

How to find us	Address:
	Telephone number:
	Opening times:

Unit 8 The country park (Sessions 3 and 4) • **Skill:** writing a brochure
Ask the children to complete the sentences about what you can do in the country park. For the next session, ask them to draw a map and complete the address, telephone number and opening times.

UNIT 9

The kingdom under the sea

Story about a fantasy world

Introduction

In this unit, children talk about the setting for a story, prior to watching the teacher model the writing of a fantasy story.

Linked text: 'Olly the octopus' (Big Book).

TARGET
- write a story with a basic beginning, middle and ending
- write simple sentences

PUPIL TARGET
- I can write a story

OUTCOME
- a story about the kingdom under the sea

NLS OBJECTIVES

Y1 T3 T12   to apply phonological, graphic knowledge and sight vocabulary to spell words accurately

Y1 T3 T14   to write stories using simple settings

SCOTTISH 5–14 GUIDELINES
- Imaginative writing
- Punctuation and structure
- Spelling

Session 1

You will need
- Big Book pages 36–37
- Post-it notes and marker pen
- Copies of PCM 17
- A card bubble for each child (optional)

(Big Book illustration labelled: Olly, Nipper, The King of the Sea — "The kingdom under the sea")

Talk for writing

- Ask the children to hold up their bubble (optional) and look at the picture on Big Book pages 36–37 while you take them on an imaginary trip to the bottom of the sea. Talk through what's happening in the picture, as this gives them clues to the story that follows.

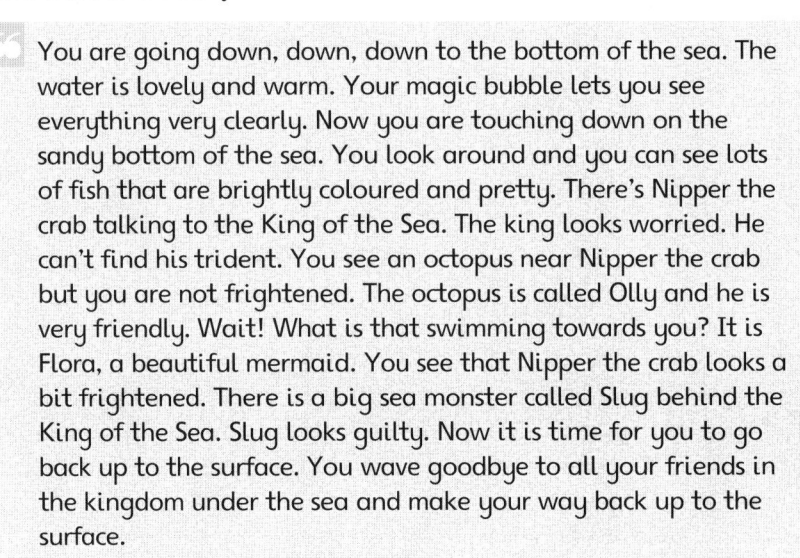

> You are going down, down, down to the bottom of the sea. The water is lovely and warm. Your magic bubble lets you see everything very clearly. Now you are touching down on the sandy bottom of the sea. You look around and you can see lots of fish that are brightly coloured and pretty. There's Nipper the crab talking to the King of the Sea. The king looks worried. He can't find his trident. You see an octopus near Nipper the crab but you are not frightened. The octopus is called Olly and he is very friendly. Wait! What is that swimming towards you? It is Flora, a beautiful mermaid. You see that Nipper the crab looks a bit frightened. There is a big sea monster called Slug behind the King of the Sea. Slug looks guilty. Now it is time for you to go back up to the surface. You wave goodbye to all your friends in the kingdom under the sea and make your way back up to the surface.

UNIT 9

The kingdom under the sea

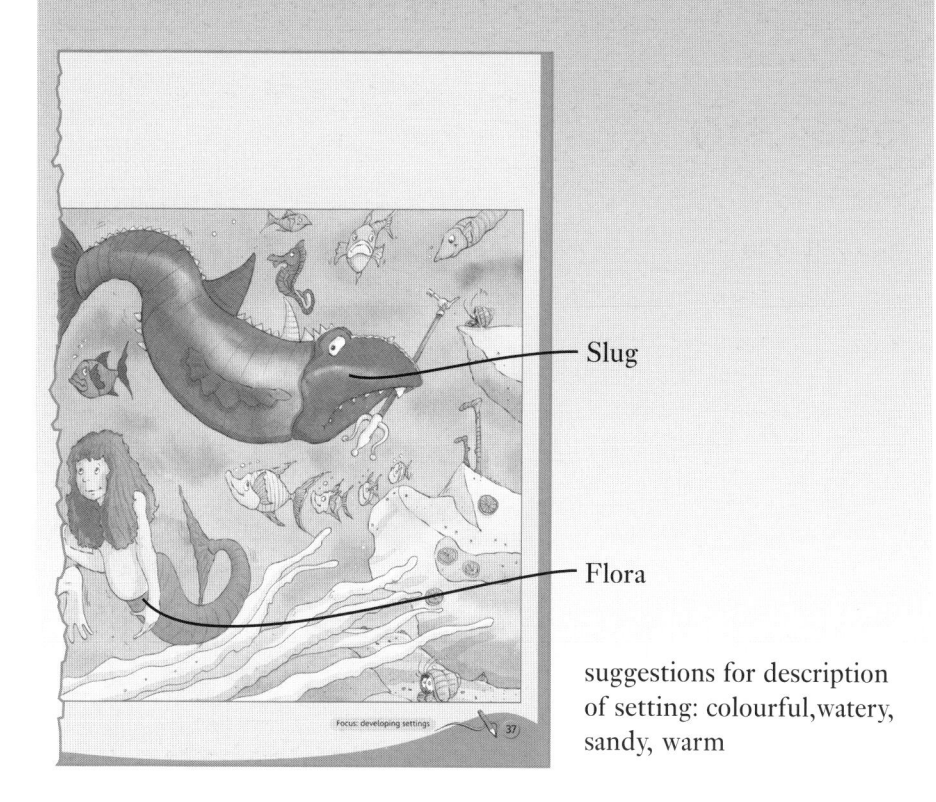

- Slug
- Flora

suggestions for description of setting: colourful, watery, sandy, warm

Shared writing

Teacher demonstration/Teacher scribing

- Write some labels on Post-its for the characters that the children saw on their adventure under the sea, e.g. Flora, Olly, Nipper, the King of the Sea and Slug the sea monster. Talk through the writing process, particularly the use of capital letters for the names. Invite individual children to come out and to fix the label close to the picture of the character.

- Now do the same for the setting, asking the children to suggest adjectives to describe the scene.

Group work

- PCM 17 Ask the children to label the characters and write words to describe the scene.

Rounding up

- Take the character labels off the Big Book. Give out the labels to individual children. Any child who has a label should read the label and then tell the rest of the class something about themselves, e.g. "I am Flora and I am a mermaid", "I am the King of the Sea and I have lost my magic trident."

UNIT 9
The kingdom under the sea

Session 2

You will need
- Big Book pages 38–40
- Flip chart or white board and marker pen

The missing trident

Down, down, down under the sea was a magic kingdom. The King of the Sea lived there. One day the king could not find his magic trident.

'Have you seen my trident?' asked the king. 'No, I haven't,' said Nipper.

Talk for writing

- Look at pages 38–40 of the Big Book. Read the story to the children. Look at the six pictures and help the children to connect the narrative.

- Ask questions to trigger information about the characters, e.g.

  > Why is the King of the Sea angry? What has naughty Slug done? What can Olly see? What does the King of the Sea do?

- Encourage the children to shape their answers into full sentences, e.g. "The King of the Sea is angry because someone has taken his magic trident."

Plan for writing

- On the flip chart, write the heading 'Characters' and ask the children if they can remember all the characters in 'The missing trident'.

- Ask the children to think of words to describe each character, and write these on the flip chart. Prompt with questions such as "Who was cross?" and "How do you think Slug behaved?" Encourage the children to look for evidence in the story.

Group work

- Ask the children to choose a character, talk about it with a partner and then role-play what the characters do in the story. (Adult help required.)

Rounding up

- Ask the children to share their role-plays from the group work.

Session 3

You will need
- Big Book pages 38–41
- Copies of PCM 18
- Acetate sheet and marker pen

Unit 9 — The kingdom under the sea

The King of the Sea, Flora and Nipper went to find Olly.
'Have you seen my trident?' asked the king.
'Have you asked Slug?' asked Olly.

'Slug, have you seen my trident?' asked the king.
'Umm, well, no,' said Slug slowly.

Slug is trying to hide something

Plan for writing

Teacher demonstration/Teacher scribing

- Tell the children that you are going to write a plan for 'The missing trident'. Look again at the six pictures which tell the story and ensure that all the children can follow the plot.

- Look at the story plan on page 41 of the Big Book. Under the heading 'Setting' talk about all the things the children 'saw' when they went on their underwater adventure. Scribe these on the acetate sheet.

- Ask the children to help you to map the events of the story under the headings 'Beginning', 'Middle' and 'End'. Use questions to support the children's answers, e.g. "What happened at the beginning of the story?" Encourage them to sequence the events of the story accurately. Write the events under the subheadings on the acetate sheet.

UNIT 9

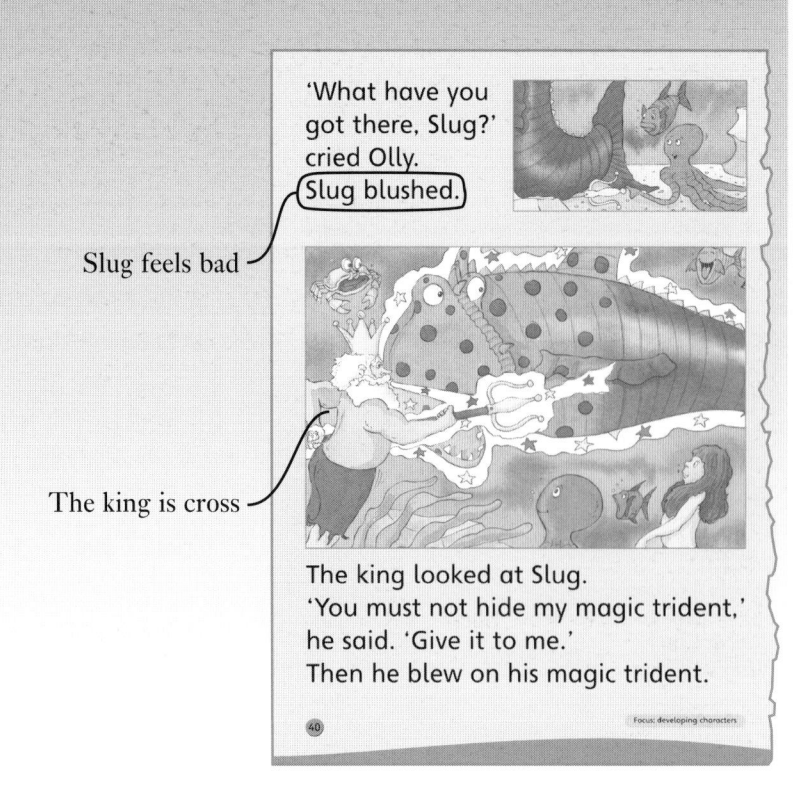

The kingdom under the sea

'What have you got there, Slug?' cried Olly.
Slug blushed.

Slug feels bad

The king is cross

The king looked at Slug.
'You must not hide my magic trident,' he said. 'Give it to me.'
Then he blew on his magic trident.

Group work

- PCM 18 This is a frame for a story plan for 'The missing trident'. Ask the children to decide what information goes under each heading, 'Beginning', 'Middle' and 'End' and to complete the story plan.

Rounding up

- Ask some children to talk through their plans, explaining how they structured the story.
- Talk about how different types of stories start. What would be a good way to start a fantasy story like this? E.g. 'Down, down, down under the sea...'

Session 4

UNIT 9
The kingdom under the sea

story plan:
- Setting: Deep, deep down under the sea.
- Beginning: The King of the Sea could not find his magic trident.
- Middle: The king asked Nipper and Olly if they had seen his trident.
- End: The king blew on his trident.

You will need
- Big Book pages 38–41
- Notes on acetate sheet from Session 3
- Copies of PCM 18 from Session 3
- Flip chart and marker pen
- Children's white boards and pens
- Blank paper (to cover up text)

Shared writing

Teacher demonstration
- Cover up the text on the Big Book pages 38–40.
- Explain to the children that you are now ready to write the story of 'The missing trident'. You are going to refer to the plan that you completed in the previous session, on page 41 of the Big Book.
- Talk to the children about how to start a fantasy story. Remind them that it should be a magical experience for readers, so you will start:

  > Down, down, down under the sea was a magic kingdom. The King of the Sea lived there. One day the king could not find his magic trident.

- Talk through the writing process as you write on the flip chart. Think aloud to share with the children the decisions you are making about your writing.
- Look at the remaining pictures and ask the children to help you decide what to write. Orally rehearse each sentence before you write it. Incorporate relevant spelling work as you write words, either by inviting the children to spell a particular word on their whiteboards or by asking them to tell you what letter to write to start a word.

Supported composition
- Ask the children to write a sentence to go with one of the pictures.

Group work
- PCM 18 Ensure that each child has their copy of the PCM from Session 3. Ask the children to use their story plan to write the part of the story when Olly sees that Slug is trying to hide the king's magic trident.

Rounding up
- Ask some children to share their stories from the group work.

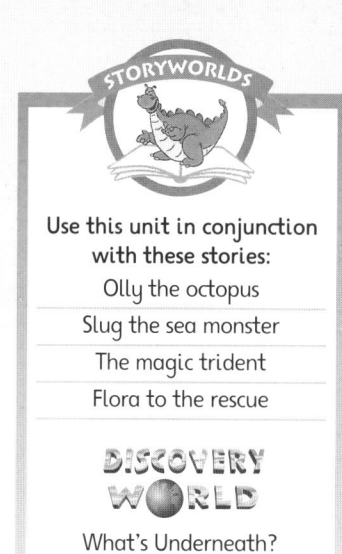

STORYWORLDS

Use this unit in conjunction with these stories:
- Olly the octopus
- Slug the sea monster
- The magic trident
- Flora to the rescue

DISCOVERY WORLD
What's Underneath? (report)

Name

The kingdom under the sea

Label the pictures and write words to describe the kingdom under the sea.

Name _____

The missing trident

Complete the story plan.

Beginning

_____
_____

Slug

Flora

Middle

_____
_____

The King of the Sea

Olly

End

_____
_____

Nipper

Unit 9 The kingdom under the sea (Sessions 3 and 4) • **Skill:** completing a story plan
Ask the children to complete the story plan. In Session 4, ask the children to use their plan to write the part of the story when Olly sees that Slug has the king's trident.

UNIT 10

The Gingerbread Man
Traditional story

Introduction
In this unit, children re-visit the traditional tale of 'The Gingerbread Man'. They sequence the events of the story and consider the events from the point of view of different characters.

Linked texts:
'Once Upon a Time World' stories, Stage 6.

TARGET
- begin to rehearse sentences before writing

PUPIL TARGET
- I can re-tell a traditional tale

OUTCOME
- a story book

NLS OBJECTIVES
Y1 T3 T13   to write about significant incidents from known stories

Y1 T3 S3   to read familiar texts aloud with pace and expression

SCOTTISH 5–14 GUIDELINES
- Imaginative writing
- Punctuation and structure

Session 1

You will need
- Big Book pages 42–45
- Acetate sheet and marker pen
- Children's white boards and pens
- Copies of PCM 19

examples for speech bubbles:

old woman: I will make a gingerbread man.

dog: Yum, yum. You look good to eat.

> **The Gingerbread Man**
>
> Once upon a time there was a little old woman...
>
> The gingerbread man tried to get out of the oven.

Talk for writing
- Ask the children if they know what gingerbread is or if they have ever eaten a gingerbread man.
- Show the class the story of 'The Gingerbread Man' on pages 42–45 of the Big Book. Ask the children if they can remember the story. Talk through the story. Guide the children into a re-telling using appropriate language for the traditional tale, e.g. "Once upon a time…" and "Run, run, as fast as you can. You can't catch me. I'm the gingerbread man."

Shared writing

Teacher demonstration
- Look at the first picture. Explain to the children that you are going to describe what is happening in this first event in the story. Talk through the process as you do so. Write the text on the acetate sheet.

> This is the beginning of the traditional tale, so I will start with, 'Once upon a time there was a little old woman and a little old man. One day the little old woman made a gingerbread man.'

- When you have written the first caption re-read it with the children.
- Ask the children to look at the next picture. What is happening? Rehearse the language they are going to write, e.g. "The gingerbread man tried to get out of the oven."

UNIT 10

The Gingerbread Man

> Run, run, as fast as you can. You can't catch me, I'm the gingerbread man.

As quick as a flash, the gingerbread man...

The little old man and the little old woman and the dog...

} challenging descriptive language

Supported composition

- Tell the children to work with a partner and to write a sentence describing the second picture on their white boards. They should hold up their white boards when they have finished.
- Use their suggestions to write the second caption on the acetate sheet below the second picture. Continue until all the pictures have captions.

Group work

- PCM 19 Enlarge the PCM to A3 size, then ask the children to write captions for the pictures in the mini-book. (Adult help required.)

Rounding up

- Ask individual children to read out their captions from the group work.

UNIT 10
The Gingerbread Man

Session 2

You will need
- Big Book pages 42–45
- Copies of PCM 20
- Children's white boards and pens
- Four pieces of white card for speech bubbles
- 4 labels for 'old woman', 'gingerbread man', 'horse', 'fox'

Then the horse began to chase the gingerbread man.

Just then…

Talk for writing

- Talk with the children about the characters in the story. Remind them of the gingerbread man's refrain and recite it together.

Shared writing

Teacher demonstration/Teacher scribing

- Tell the children that you are going to add speech bubbles to the story so that you can fill in what the characters are saying. Remind the children that in speech bubbles you just write the actual words a character speaks.

- Look at the first picture on page 42 of the Big Book. Begin by asking the children to suggest what the old woman might be saying. Listen to the children's contributions. When you are happy with one that is a complete sentence and which would be spoken by the old woman, then write it on a speech bubble and stick it next to the old woman. Talk through the writing process as you do it, explaining what you are doing.

- Do the same with the dog, the horse and the fox. Bring in relevant sentence and word level work, e.g.

> Who knows how I must start my sentence? What sound can you hear at the beginning of the word 'gingerbread'? Can you all write the word 'man' on your white boards?

UNIT 10
The Gingerbread Man

Then the sly fox saw his chance to trick the gingerbread man.

The gingerbread man climbed on the fox's nose. SNAP! SNAP! SNAP! went the fox.

examples for speech bubbles:

horse: Yum, yum. You look good to eat.

fox: Climb up on my back.

Supported composition
- Ask the children to write some speech for the gingerbread man on their white boards.

Group work
- PCM 20 This shows the old woman, the gingerbread man, the horse and the fox. Each character has an empty speech bubble. Tell the children to write something that each character said in the story.

Rounding up
- Play a guessing game with the children. Tell them that you are going to say things that characters in the story said. They have to guess which character said those words. Lay out the four character labels on the floor, with space between them. Tell the children to stand round the label of the character who said the words you have spoken, e.g.

> "Yum, yum, you look good to eat." "I will give him a cherry nose." "You can't catch me." "Let me help you cross the river." "I will make a gingerbread man." "Climb up on my back."

Unit 10
The Gingerbread Man

Session 3

You will need

- Big Book pages 42–47
- Flip chart or white board and marker pen

cosy, happy scene

Talk for writing

- Ask the children what happens at the end of the story. Does anyone feel sorry for the gingerbread man? Was it fair that the fox ate him?

Shared writing

Teacher demonstration

- Tell the class to look at the picture on pages 46–47 of the Big Book. It shows what might have happened to the gingerbread man if he had not run away and been eaten by the fox. Ask the children what is happening in the picture (the old woman and the old man are happily doing a jigsaw with the gingerbread man and they are all friends together). Tell the children that you are going to write a story to tell this different version of 'The Gingerbread Man', so first you must make some notes.

- Look back at the story on pages 42–45 and decide where your new story should start, e.g. before the gingerbread man runs away. On the flip chart, make notes with the children under the headings, 'Setting', 'Characters', 'Beginning', 'Middle' and 'End'.

Group work

- Ask the children to talk about why the gingerbread man might stay with the old man and woman. (Adult help required.)

Rounding up

- Discuss good phrases to use to start and finish traditional stories. What might they write at the end of the new version of 'The Gingerbread Man'?

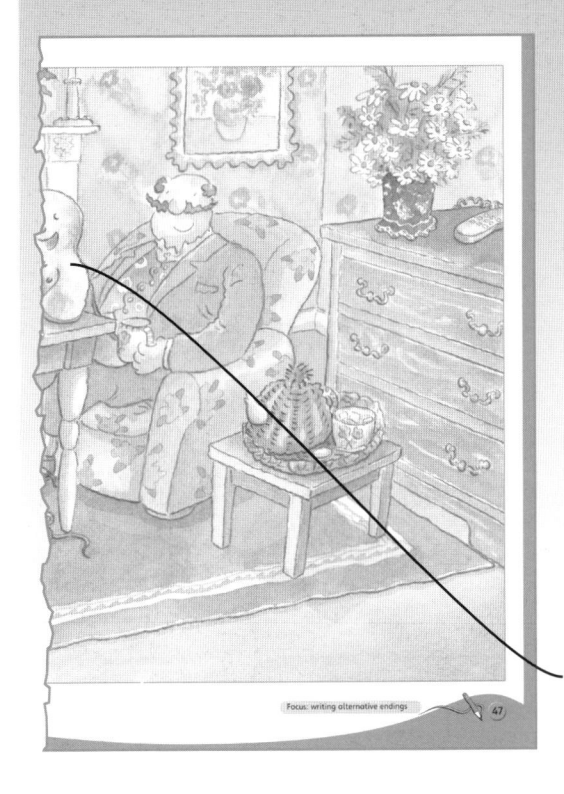

Session 4

You will need
- Big Book pages 46–47
- Notes from Session 3
- Flip chart or white board and marker pen

the gingerbread man is happy

UNIT **10**
The Gingerbread Man

Talk for writing

- Look at pages 46–47 of the Big Book. Ask the children to remind you of the alternative version of the story that you talked about in Session 3.

Shared writing

Teacher demonstration/Teacher scribing

- Show the children the notes that you prepared yesterday. Write the story with them, asking the children for suggestions.

  > How shall we start our story? What's a good way to start a traditional tale? Yes, let's write, 'Once upon a time…' Where do we need to start our new version? I'll go back to the point when the old woman took the gingerbread man out of the oven. Let's write, ' "Good, now we can eat him," said the old man.' What might the gingerbread man say?

- Continue scribing the story with the children, looking back at the notes from Session 3.

Group work

- Ask the children to write the new ending of 'The Gingerbread Man'. Encourage them to finish their story with 'and they lived happily ever after.'

Rounding up

- Share some of the children's stories and discuss whether they prefer the original version of the story, or their new version with the happy ending.

Use this unit in conjunction with these stories:
The Gingerbread Man
The Princess and the Pea
The Old Woman and the Vinegar Bottle
The Cooking Pot

83

Name

The Gingerbread Man

Write captions for the pictures.

Unit 10 The Gingerbread Man (Session 1) • Skill: writing a book
Enlarge the PCM to A3 size. Ask the children to write captions for each of the pictures including the title page and then help them to fold the paper into a zig-zag book.

Name

What did they say?

Write in the speech bubbles.

Unit 10 The Gingerbread Man (Session 2) • **Skill:** writing speech bubbles
Ask the children to write in the speech bubbles something that each character said.